Entrepreneur® **MENTOR** SERIES

CONSULTING

*The Business That Generates
Mega Dollars and Puts
You in Control of Your
Financial Future*

MARC KRAMER

EP
Entrepreneur®
Press

Editorial Director: Jere Calmes
Cover Design: Beth Hanson-Winter
Composition: CWL Publishing Enterprises, www.cwlpub.com

This publication is designed to provide accurate and authorita-
tive information in regard to the subject matter covered. It is sold
with the understanding that the publisher is not engaged in rendering legal, accounting, or other professional services. If legal
advice or other expert assistance is required, the services of a
competent professional person should be sought.
—From a Declaration of Principles jointly adopted by a
Committee of the American Bar Association and
a Committee of Publishers and Associations

ISBN 1-891984-97-7

Printed in Canada

09 08 07 06 05 04 03   10 9 8 7 6 5 4 3 2 1

Contents

PREFACE

About a year and a half ago, I was talking to my editor, Jere Calmes, for whom I have written two books, about the lack of loyalty businesses have for their employees today. Companies like Dell, Cisco, and ATT, that are sitting on mountains of cash, abandon their people at the first sign of economic trouble. Whatever happened to waiting out the storm? When times are good, they can't understand why employees leave for higher-paying jobs with competitors.

The reason most people leave is not just for the jump in salary. They leave because they know when the going gets rough the company will get going and possibly lay people off. Professionals who have been through a couple of economic down cycles have learned that it is best to make and save as much as you can because the company won't stand by you when sales soften.

I suggested to Jere that I write a book about starting a consulting practice and call it "Risk Averse? Become a Consultant." Jere wondered whether there was more risk in going out on your own than in working for someone and getting that bimonthly paycheck. Ask the million-plus white-collar workers at the various name-brand companies that have been let go in the past year how safe they felt.

Why Did I Become a Consultant?

What pushed me into consulting was the following course of events. I had left a safe job running a large regional trade association to become president of a technology company. Within a year of running the company, the owner decided to sell it, so I was back looking for a job.

A short time later, I received an offer to be a partner at US Web, which, at the time, was the largest Internet consulting firm in the world. Three months after I joined US Web, top management decided to close our office and I was asked to consider moving to Boston. I decided not to do it. They eventually shut down that location as well.

My wife, who is risk-averse, said to me that I was better off going out on my own than trust our family's future to another employer. This appealed to me as well because I am somewhat risk-averse. In my mind, the old adage that "there is safety in numbers" is a perfect way of saying why someone should go into consulting.

A successful consultant doesn't take on one or two clients; he or she takes on five to 10 clients, which spreads out his or her risk. In one year, one of my clients was acquired, another client, a New York Stock Exchange company, was broken up and sold for its various business units, and another client went bankrupt. Each of those companies had offered me a full-time senior-level position.

All I could think of when I received those offers was that I was putting my family's welfare in jeopardy. As my practice grew, my wife wouldn't hear of me even considering working for someone else. She said that for the first time in our 17 years of marriage, she felt financially secure. My children, who are ages 11 and 8, liked seeing dad every day.

Should You Become a Consultant?

According to statistics, getting into consulting is not difficult, and your chances of success in consulting are higher than building a company that requires outside capital.

According to the U.S. Bureau of Labor and Statistics, the consulting market profile is as follows:

- 6.8 million full-time consultants
- 25 million part-time consultants
- 53% are owned by men
- 90% of the market is white-collar workers
- 90% use a computer for the work they do

The number of consultants is growing 6% annually

- Between $50,000 and $500,000 in annual sales
- Average age of small office/home office (SOHO) worker is 50
- 80% are married
- 47% have dependent children
- 69% of household income comes from business
- 53% have household incomes of $100,000 and/or net worth of $500,000 or more
- 24% own multiple SOHO businesses
- Average length of business 17 years

According to SOHO Jobs (www.sohojobs.org), the top occupations of consultants are as follows:

- Attorney
- Business training
- Children's products and programs
- Environmental consultant
- Event planner and organizer
- Financial planner
- Home inspector

- Home repairs and landscaping
- Internet sales and marketing
- Internet Web master
- Marketing
- Personal coach
- Sales
- Software development
- Technical support
- Virtual/personal assistant

The personal characteristics of consultants are very similar to those of any entrepreneur:

- Committed to success
- Risk-takers
- Self-motivated
- Self-disciplined
- Patient
- Attracted to flexibility and adaptability
- Willing to sacrifice
- Hard workers
- Handle stress well

Why Write Another Consulting Book?

The next logical question is, with so many consulting books out there, why write another one? The publishing community works very much like the venture capital community. For the most part, publishers look for concepts that have big markets, which increases the chances of having a successful book. Publishers require a proposal that mirrors a business plan. They want to know who would buy it, average income of buyer, publications that would potentially promote it, a competitive analysis of similar books, the writer's expertise, and a detailed outline of the book.

Many people I knew who got into consulting complained that there weren't any really substantive books on how to start a consulting practice. They wanted a book that would take them step by step through the process of building a successful consulting practice—developing business and marketing plans, deciding how to develop strategic partnerships, knowing what to say on a client call (because many of them have no sales experience), building a Web site, knowing which organizations to join, and developing additional lines of revenue.

Consultants said they wanted books that didn't just give them an outline of a business or marketing plan, but actually gave them a sample plan. They wanted a step-by-step methodology and process for obtaining sales. They wanted to know what marketing concepts work and which ones they shouldn't waste their money on.

My book walks you through every step that will allow you to be a successful consultant. You will read advice from marketing, sales, and technology consultants and throughout the book you will read question-and-answer interviews with other successful consultants in a variety of fields about the best ways to market, sell, and build your consulting practice.

Once you get a few clients and can pay your bills you will start to feel intellectually challenged. It won't take long until you start to make the same amount of money you were making working for someone, but without the pressure of worrying about you or the company making its quarterly financial forecasts. Within a year to a year in half, you probably will be making more money than you ever made in your life.

There will be clients who will ask you to work for them. Don't fall into that trap. Think about all the nonsense you go through interviewing for a job and either not getting it or getting it, but being let go through no fault of your own. Why put you and your family through that? Take control of your financial future! If you have any questions, e-mail me at marc@kramercommunications.com.

Dedication and Acknowledgments

I dedicate this book to my father, Robert Kramer, who spent many hours editing my writing when I began my career as a sports journalist at age 15. My dad always encouraged my writing and was willing to drive anywhere if someone was willing to publish my works. He was even more excited when my articles came out than I was. I have worked very hard at trying to emulate him as a father.

Secondarily, I want to thank my wife and daughters, who had to put up with many vacations where I spent the mornings writing. I want to thank Gail Jones for editing my manuscript and John Woods and his company, CWL Publishing Enterprises, Inc. for turning the manuscript into the book you're now reading. Finally, I want to thank my editor and friend, Jere Calmes, for whom I have written three books. Jere is the best editor anyone can work with because he gives you quality feedback, but doesn't try to change your style.

Anyone who reads this book and would like to contact me, please e-mail me at marc@kramercommunications.com.

SHOULD I BECOME A CONSULTANT?

THINGS TO THINK ABOUT WHEN STRIKING OUT ON YOUR OWN ◄

When I was a teenager, a friend's father left the company that had employed him for 20 years and started a marketing consulting practice. I came from a family of business owners, but I had never met or heard of someone starting a consulting practice, let alone knew what a consultant did. My friend told me his father worked at home and provided advice to companies on how best to market their products or services.

I thought, "What a great job!" You get paid to work at home and dispense words of wisdom. From the looks of my friend's house and the car his father was driving, I decided that one day I wanted to be like my friend's father.

Now that I have been a consultant for five years, I have learned that consulting provides a better lifestyle and more economic freedom than I initially thought, but I also underestimated the amount of time required to be successful. As you enter the world of consulting, you should be aware of the pluses and minuses of the profession.

Pluses

There are five pluses to being a consultant.

Financial Security—The only person who can fire or lay you off is you. If you work hard and provide a quality service you will not only earn a living, but a very good one. You will be able to secure your financial future. I had a client who retained me to be his outsourced chief marketing officer. We signed a contract for a year, and six months into the contract he lost several major clients and had to cancel my contract. I told my wife that I am thankful I work for myself and have five other clients, because I hate interviewing for new positions.

Time Control—One of the best perks of being a consultant is that you have more control over your time. You can tell a client that you don't work on Thursday afternoons because you coach your daughter's soccer team or play in the community orchestra. Not many companies are flexible about how people use their time and, in most cases, you have to give your employer advance notice.

Variety of Clients—Many people get bored and lose their edge because they only work for one company.

Budget Control—One of the most irritating and frustrating parts of working for someone else is having to get approval on expenditures. True, most executives have some latitude on how they spend their budgets, but there are usually guidelines and rules to follow that you don't always agree with.

Vacation Control—I hated being limited to when and how much vacation I could take. When you work for someone else, if you don't sign up quickly enough for those weeks when your children and spouse are also available, you may

Time to Make a Change?

A friend of mine was chief marketing officer of an international company. After working 12-hour days for six months he decided to take his family to the Caribbean. He left instructions that he should be called only if there was an emergency. Two days after he arrived, the CEO tracked him down to discuss the marketing strategy for a new product that was going to be launched six months from the day they were speaking. My friend ended up on the telephone two different times for two hours each. Finally, the CEO stopped calling. When my friend came back, he found out that the CEO had turned over the reins of his group to another person and told my friend he needed fresh thinking and that it was time to make a change.

not be able to take a vacation with your family if the only possible time for that turns out to be the same period requested by many other people. It is usually the case that company policy prohibits many people being away at the same time. Practically everyone has spent part of every vacation answering electronic and voice mail or doing work. Does the company reward you with extra vacation days for taking work on vacation with you? No!

Minuses

There are only five minuses and I find only two of them annoying: paying taxes and benefits, and constantly worrying about finding clients.

Client Acquisition—The biggest concern for most consultants is how to get clients. You know you can do the work, but you are used to having a sales force bring in the business and then work your magic. I look at client acquisition as a small price to pay for my freedom and peace of mind. True, it is a constant worry, but so is losing your job for reasons you have no direct control over.

Taxes and Benefits—No one who goes into consulting is prepared for the sticker shock of paying $12,000 or more for family health insurance if one's spouse isn't working and having a company provide coverage. Who wants to pay the 6 percent of unemployment insurance, or the life insurance, or the paid vacations, or the car that a company used to pay for? Most people who enter consulting will find that in a relatively short period of time they are making more money than they ever made in their lives and, therefore, will have to pay obscene quarterly federal, state, and local taxes. I like the idea of paying more taxes, however, because that means I am successful.

Lack of Camaraderie—Many people look forward to seeing their comrades at the office. They like the interaction and the ability to bounce ideas off of coworkers. Most of us also like feeling we are part of a group. In the beginning, being on one's own takes some getting used to, but then you realize that you can replace those relationships through your clients and business organizations you join.

Collecting Fees—Although I typically collect half of my fees upfront, I find that one of the most frustrating parts of

Getting Paid

A client of mine hired me to write a business plan and to assist the company in raising money. We signed a $15,000 contract. The contract called for me to receive $10,000 to write the plan and $5,000 to assist in raising capital. I was paid $5,000 upfront, and the contract stipulated that I would be paid $2,500 on delivery of a draft document and the remaining $2,500 on delivery of the final document, which would trigger upfront payment of $5,000 for assisting in raising capital. As a consultant you count on clients fulfilling their contracts in order to manage your own cash flow. After finishing the draft of the plan, however, the client informed me that he was having financial difficulties and, as this book is published, I have never had the opportunity to finish that contract.

being a consultant is getting clients to fulfill their contracts and collecting on those contracts.

24/7/365—No matter where you go or what you do, you are constantly worried about taking care of existing clients and finding new ones. The business never gives you a break, but I am willing to live with that in exchange for knowing I have a lot more control over my professional and financial future without the uncertainty of working for someone else.

Before you decide whether to become a consultant, you might consider going through some career testing. I interviewed Dr. Paul Brooks, who provides career testing with Manchester International, Inc. He brings to his work a strong background in the discovery, design, and delivery of human capital management solutions. And he is an expert in career and vocational counseling, training, coaching, performance management, personnel selection, and departure systems, as well as assessment design and validation.

Dr. Brooks holds a Ph.D. in Industrial-Organizational Psychology from Illinois Institute of Technology, Chicago, Illinois. He is a member of the American Psychological Association (APA) and Society for Industrial-Organizational Psychology (SIOP). He has practiced applied psychology for human capital solutions for 12 years, consulting with large organizations such as Household International, LaSalle Banks, the City of Chicago, and Roadway Express.

Question: What type of test should someone take before starting a consulting business to find out whether to go out on his or her own?

Response: Perhaps it is best to first define a test. A test is a collection of questions, tasks, or actual behaviors designed to predict some type of outcome. Examples would include specific tests of knowledge (e.g., certification exams, licensing exams, and subject mastery), skills and abilities (e.g., mechanical aptitude, eye—hand coordination, basic accounting, and general business intelligence). Combining several tests into a test battery drastically improves prediction.

Currently there are very few, if any, tests designed specifically to predict success in a startup consulting business. Test-makers design assessments for large markets such as college entrance exams and pre-employment tests but not for starting a consulting business. Because these tests are not available, decision makers tend to develop content-based assessments.

Question: How do we identify entrepreneurial talent?

Response: Ideally, a group of successful consultants will get together and identify factors they think contributed to their success. Alternatively researchers look at case studies of successful consultants and infer which attributes are most important for success. These types of investigations are often termed *surveys*, *quizzes*, or *assessments*. Review of these nonscientific assessments reveals an overarching factor called "entrepreneurial talent."

Question: What traits are typically found in people who have the greatest chance of becoming a successful entrepreneur?

Response: Compelling evidence suggests that certain traits are associated with entrepreneurial success: openness to new experiences, responsiveness, flexibility, talent for pleasant social transactions, and goal direction. Moreover, previous life experiences have also been linked to entrepreneurial success such as experience with risk-taking, the need for achievement, and the need to acquire and exercise power.

Entrepreneur Self-Assessment

Starting a business should always begin with self-assessment, according to Paul Brooks. Entrepreneurs who follow a path of self-discovery may find that they improve the likelihood of their success. Now the question becomes, what assessment should I use? Studies have identified the following five character traits as having strong potential to predict future success in an entrepreneurial environment. Let's look at these and the comments of Paul Brooks on each one.

1. **Open to New Experiences**

   Because entrepreneurs are imaginative and curious, with wide-ranging intellects, they tend to be explorers. Open to new approaches and intrigued by innovation, they tend to forge ahead into uncharted territories. Entrepreneurs tend to be responsive, by modifying their behavior to fit the situation. They tend to be cool, calm, and collected in most all situations.

2. **Mixed Sociability**

   Depending on the situation, entrepreneurs do have the ability to work in isolation and to be outgoing and social. They are termed 'ambiverts.' They can be a leader or a player, accepting the demands of each role.

3. **Dependability**

   Entrepreneurs tend to be goal directed. They target a place they want to be in the future and determine the best means of reaching it. They tend to be persistent and hardworking once they've established a target.

4. **Agreeableness**

   Often lone wolves, entrepreneurs tend to follow their own judgments rather than group consensus. They tend to seek and exercise power. As challengers, they tend to offer alternative viewpoints to group-think.

5. **Need for Achievement**

Entrepreneurs tend to be risk-takers in their efforts to achieve their goal. Success is the goal and the path to the goal is risky. To be a visionary means accepting and taking risks, tempered by desire and tenacity.

Now that you know the pluses and minuses of being a consultant and you have read what a top expert on starting a business advises on assessing whether you are ready to go out on your own, you really need to ask yourself the following ten questions before making the leap.

Ten Questions to Ask Yourself When Considering Becoming a Consultant

1. Is there a market for my service? Before you leave your current job to strike out on your own, you need to determine whether there is a big enough market for your expertise that can match your income from your current employer. A business colleague of mine with expertise in a narrowly defined area of aerospace engineering worked at General Electric Aerospace. When we got together socially, he would remark how lucky I was to be able to work out of my home and that he was thinking of leaving GEA to go out on his own. One of the first questions I asked him was who else besides GEA would buy his expertise? Unfortunately, he couldn't come back with a quick answer because there are only two governments funding space programs and one of them doesn't share its expertise with other governments. Most importantly, only one buyer valued his expertise.

2. How crowded is the market? Before you start your consulting practice, find out how many people offer your service in your geographic region and determine the demand. A few years ago, if you were selling SAP or Web site development consulting services, you needed to clone yourself ten times over. The demand was much greater than the supply. The consultants in this area were making hundreds of thousands of dollars each year. When other smart, technically savvy people started to learn these specialties, the price for these services dropped dramatically. As the need leveled off, many consultants found they couldn't get work. If the consultants in your region are considering taking full-time jobs, then you know the field is either overcrowded or the demand isn't there.

3. Do I have the discipline to be a consultant? Every weekday I get up at 5:15 A.M. and ride my bike or go to the gym, have breakfast, and promptly start my work at 7 A.M. and stop at 6 P.M. On Saturday, I start at 7 A.M. and stop at 10 A.M. and work a full day on Sundays. I take certain holidays off, but my life is very structured. Many people mistakenly believe that being a consultant means you can work at your leisure. As you will find from reading this book and hearing what other consultants have to say, you need to be highly disciplined or you will be out of business.

Friends joke with me about watching soap operas and wearing out the refrigerator door, and I admit that it is very easy to fall into the trap of kicking back and saying I am my own boss so I will get the work done whenever it suits me. Unfortunately, consultants have only their time to sell and every hour wasted on nonbillable activities is lost income and opportunity, not to mention being unable to finish projects early, or at least on time. If you are the type of person who can't develop and stick to a routine and avoid unnecessary distractions, you will fail as a consultant.

4. Can I handle working alone? Unless you are working with a partner (which I will address later in this book), you will probably be working in your home office or at a shared-office facility. Many people I know go to a mall just so they can be around people. Before I was a consultant and worked for other companies, there were always people who felt the urge to knock on my door or stop by my cubicle to shoot the breeze. If you are a person who needs daily contact with other people, consulting can be isolating. I enjoy interacting with people, but I have always been someone who didn't like studying with others and preferred an office with a door rather than working in an open space.

5. Can I handle the pressure of not having a steady paycheck? One of the most difficult adjustments for consultants is not getting a regular paycheck. Unless you receive a contract from your current employer or began laying the groundwork for your consulting practice early and obtained a contract, it will probably take from four to twelve weeks to get your first contract. During that time no money will be coming in and you are now paying for your healthcare insurance, telephone, business supplies, gasoline, and personal expenses. This lack of a regular paycheck is at the top of the list for scaring people off from starting their own consulting practices.

6. Can my spouse/significant other handle the uncertainty of my not receiving a regular paycheck? In most cases, non-married consultants can mentally talk themselves through the problem of not having a steady paycheck because they believe that the first contract of many is around the corner and they just have to keep pitching and not give up. Spouses and significant others may not be so patient. Anyone getting into consulting should check his or her mate's temperament and see what level of pain he or she can tolerate.

As I mentioned in the Preface to this book, my wife was mentally ready and actually was the driver behind my going out on my own. She watched as the business world went from long-term investments and lifetime employment to the "make it happen every day or you are out of here" mentality of corporations. She was tired of the corporate roller coaster and lack of loyalty and was willing to give up the short-term steady paycheck for long-term financial security.

7. Do I have the financial resources to support myself until my consulting practice can support me? If you have any inkling that you would like to go out on your own, you should put away enough money so that your salary is covered for one year. I have never met a competent consultant who couldn't get a contract within 90 days, yet it usually takes most consultants two to three years to make more money, including benefits, than they were making with their past employers. It's important to have a cash reserve so you can focus on building your business.

8. Do I have the sales skills or can I acquire the sales skills to successfully sell myself? Most people who go into consulting bring terrific expertise and a track record of success to what they do. What most lack are the skills to sell their capabilities. The most difficult part of consulting is selling one's services. Can you learn to sell yourself? Yes, there are many good sales training programs. It has been my experience that you have to enjoy talking about what you do and meeting people to be successful at sales. In fact, I think it is more important to be good at selling yourself than delivering your service.

9. Do I have the business contacts that will provide me access to business prospects? One of the quickest and best

A colleague of mine started a consulting firm specializing in transportation logistics because his employer, on the advice of a consultant, had decided to eliminate my colleague's group. Fortunately for my colleague, the employer was going to need help transitioning to an outsource group and my friend demonstrated to his former employer that he would be the ideal outsourced "chief logistics officer." He ended up receiving a monthly retainer to work with vendors to manage logistics.

ways to build a consulting practice is to network with friends and business associates. Take all of those business cards you have collected over the years, put them into a database, and let those people know what you are doing. If you haven't been developing a database or have a desk drawer full of business cards that haven't been entered into a database, you need to begin that process. Referral from business associates will be infinitely more important and effective than using any other marketing tool such as direct marketing, advertising, or public relations.

10. Can I handle rejection? The one thing you can be assured of is that more companies will not be interested in what you are offering than will be. If your skin isn't thick enough to handle rejection, you won't make it in consulting. You can't take it personally. I have been rejected initially by prospects who then turned around and either retained me a year later or provided an introduction to another prospect.

Interview with a Successful Consultant

Gary Samartino, who has been a consultant for over 15 years, has a degree in English from Villanova University and is President of InfoVentions, a company that provides technical writing services for large financial institutions such as The Vanguard Group and technology companies such as Unisys. Here are his thoughts on being a consultant.

Question: Why did you become a consultant?

Response: I always knew I wanted my own business, partly because my dad had his own business and he was my role model. I like the freedom of making my own decisions, and having the trust of my clients to make those decisions.

Question: How much money did it take to start your consulting practice?

Response: It took about $30,000. I took a voluntary layoff from my past employer and that is what I had to live on. Of course, later on as we grew, we had to tap a substantial line of credit at times.

Question: Did you write a business plan for yourself?

Response: Yes, I did. Since my business is fairly focused and straightforward, it's been simple to follow, and it hasn't needed much updating.

Question: How long have you been a consultant?

Response: I have been a consultant for 15 years, but I always felt like a consultant, even as an employee of other companies. I took each job looking to do the best job I could and, in doing so, gain valuable experience. Once I realized I couldn't grow in the position any longer, I would move on to another job.

Question: What is the best part of being a consultant?

Response: The freedom to do what you want when you want. Of course, you have obligations to your clients and now I have employees and I have to help them get their work done. You are never really free. I like making decisions and doing a quality job for our clients.

Question: What is the worst part of being a consultant?

Response: The amount of time it takes. It does take a toll on your personal life. It takes a lot more time than a 9-to-5 job. Sometimes it takes 50 percent to 100 percent more time. Another drawback is the anxiety of having to get clients. It's not a constant thing, but it is a major concern. However, I'd much rather put up with that anxiety than work for someone else.

Question: What is the hardest part of being a consultant?

Response: The hardest part for me is business development. It's not that it is hard, but it's hard for me to get to. Over the years I have developed a lot more confidence in getting business. In the beginning it was tough because I didn't know what I was doing. I went to Sandler Institute, which helps train people in sales. They develop an approach for performing sales tasks. They point out what techniques and attitudes work. Their whole point is to mold their tools to your personality. Sales come down to personality and trust. You need to be yourself. The really good salespeople are themselves. They don't try to sell people something they don't need. Forget the techniques. If you have that approach you will be fine. You have to believe in what you are selling.

Question: What do you like best about your work?

Response: I like writing and explaining things. It's sort of like problem solving. My consulting allows me to do that. I get the added benefit of learning about new technology and technical products, which keeps it interesting. Also, I have a lot more freedom to do quality work than I ever had as an employee. At my last full-time job, my boss used to lecture me about not being such a perfectionist and spending more time covering my butt—I couldn't handle that. And I really enjoy the people I work with. I have found terrific, self-motivated, responsible people to work with me.

Question: What do you like least about what you do?

Response: Being forced to use writing tools that are inadequate, and I'm talking mostly about Microsoft products. Using them has to add at least 25 percent to the time it takes to get projects done, and that is a conservative estimate.

Question: How did you figure what to charge your clients?

Response: At first we just made guesses. I then closely tracked each project and started to compile data on how long various projects took. Then, for new projects, I could look back at a similar one and come up with very accurate estimates for the time and materials needed for the new one. You need to meticulously track projects and the hours needed to complete them; this is critical if you are going to be profitable.

Question: How did you get your first client?

Response: We were contacting people we knew from previous jobs, and a woman I had worked with got us a project with her company.

Question: How do you market and sell yourself?

Response: Nearly all my business now comes from personal contacts and follow-up work with existing clients. For example, in the last year, I picked up two new clients through parents of other boys on my son's soccer team. Occasionally, I've had someone assist me in prospecting.

Question: How much experience do you think someone needs before they can go out and become a consultant?

Response: For my field, I would say you need at least five years of experience, and you need to have worked with several companies so that you have some diversity in that experience.

Question: How long did it take you until you were making the same salary and benefits you had when you were employed by someone else?

Response: It took about two years.

Question: Did your spouse work to support you as you grew your consulting practice?

Response: Well, not outside the home. She has worked

plenty inside the home, of course, making up for my absences.

Qustion: Do you ask for a retainer before you do your work and, if so, how much?

Response: With new clients, I do ask for a portion of the budget up front, but I usually don't get it. I try to get 25 percent to 50 percent.

Question: Have you ever had a client that refused to pay and, if so, what did you do?

Reponse: I've been very lucky; that has never happened to me. We did have one client who was having financial difficulties and didn't pay us all we were owed for a project. They tried to pay off their debt several months later, but eventually went under. But we only lost a few thousand dollars.

Question: What is the one piece of advice you would give someone wanting to become a consultant?

Response: To really enjoy the field you are going to consult in. You have to enjoy what you are doing to invest the necessary amount of time and energy consulting on your own consumes. Anyone who thinks that being a consultant will allow you to work only 20 to 30 hours a week just won't make it. If you get through the first two or three years, you should have developed enough of a work history and made enough contacts to make it for the long haul.

Chapter Key Points

I am sure you are taking deep breaths and reexamining whether you want to go out on your own, but keep the following things in mind:

🔑 You never have to worry about being fired or downsized.

🔑 There is no cap on how much money you can make.

🔑 There is no one to tell you which conferences you can and can't go to.

🔑 There is no one deciding when you can take a vacation.

🔑 You don't have to seek approval to buy that laptop you always wanted.

🔑 You don't have to work with anyone you don't want to.

DEVELOPING A BUSINESS PLAN FOR SUCCESS

MAKE SUCCESS HAPPEN ◀

Most people think of writing a business plan as an exercise to raise capital and/or as a tool to direct a group of people in building a successful enterprise. Anyone starting a full or part-time consulting practice should develop a business plan that will serve as a road map and guide for building your consulting practice. Every successful consultant I have met has taken the time to develop a business plan.

The consultants I have observed that have failed didn't take the time to write out the answers to the following five crucial questions:

- What do I plan to offer?
- Who will buy my service and what geographic region do I plan to cover?
- How will I market myself?
- Is the market saturated with what I have to offer?
- What will I charge for what I do?

What Should Be in a Business Plan?

A business plan should be a realistic view of the expectations and objectives for a business. It provides the framework within which it must operate and, ultimately, succeed or fail. For consultants, writing a business plan crystallizes your thinking and mentally prepares you for what you must do to succeed. Preparation of a comprehensive plan will not guarantee success, but lack of a sound plan will—almost certainly—ensure failure.

A formal business plan serves the following critical functions:

- helps new consultants to clarify, focus, and understand the value they can bring to their market;
- provides a well-thought-out logical framework within which consultants can develop and pursue business strategies over a specified period of time; for consultancies, there is no use planning more than a year in advance (in fact, I have found that I am updating and changing my strategy every six months because of market changes);
- serves as a basis for discussion with potential clients and strategic partners. When you are developing your consulting practice, it is a good idea to interview potential clients and strategic partners to let them know what you are planning to offer and to find out what "pains" they are currently experiencing in their business and whether your planned offering could help alleviate those problems. It is my experience that you will find out that there are more and better uses of your skills and abilities than you originally thought and that, through interviewing prospects and potential partners, you will be able to craft a better service offering and attract clients more quickly;

When I started my consulting practice I was going to focus on offering Internet marketing consulting, which meant developing marketing plans to build the visibility of any type of dot.com. Right after I began writing to business contacts about offering my services, I was told by various accountants and attorneys with whom I was dealing that my experience at writing business plans and launching new businesses was in greater demand than my skills for developing and implementing marketing plans.

- offers a benchmark against which actual performance can be measured and reviewed. You need to set certain goals for yourself, ranging from the number of prospects to whom you plan to market your service, to the appropriate strategic partners and organizations that can open doors of prospective clients, to the number and size of contracts you need to obtain to be financially self-sufficient.

The length of a business plan, including financial projections, should be between 25 and 35 single-spaced pages on average. Most business plans should contain the following:

Executive Summary. The most important section of your business plan. The executive summary is a condensed version of the business plan. The executive summary should have the following subheadings (three to four pages in length):

- *Problem/Opportunity:* The first thing you need to ask yourself is: "What problem am I solving?" After you answer that question, you need to determine whether the problem is serious enough that someone will spend money on it, regardless of the business climate. For example, companies need to improve

The Best Salespeople

A business associate of mine ran a $500 million software distributorship. He noticed that few companies had a real process for driving sales and determining which salespeople were truly stars and which ones appeared to be stars, but weren't. Most people would say the salespeople who bring in the most money are the best. My associate, however, said there were a lot of factors, ranging from the size of territory to industry focus, and that some of the best salespeople had lower sales because their targets weren't as easy to bag for a variety of reasons. The companies that used his process and methodology watched their sales go up 10 percent.

their computer infrastructure, but, as we have seen from the recent recession, companies didn't view fixing computer problems as a "must do."

- *Solution.* A description of what your company has to offer to solve the problem you just outlined.
- *Market.* A paragraph or two describing the size of the marketplace.
- *Marketing of Company.* A short description of the group(s) to whom the company will be marketed and a list of tactics you plan to use to build awareness.
- *Revenue Streams.* A description of the number of services you plan to offer and how much money each service will bring in.
- *Competition.* A one- to two-paragraph description of the competition.
- *Competitive Advantage.* Bulleted reasons why your business model is better than the competition's.
- *Capital Requirements.* The amount of money you believe you will need to get to break even and eventually become profitable.

Description of the Consultancy: A one- to three-paragraph description of the business (one page in length). In the venture capital world, this is called your "elevator pitch." Whatever service you are offering, you should be able to explain it succinctly enough that a person riding from the first to the twenty-fifth floor would have a full understanding of what you have to offer.

Objectives: The consultancy should have short-term objectives that cover years one and two and long-term objectives that start at year three and end at year five. The objectives should be quantifiable, and should focus on the following (one page in length):

- target companies you will market to in the first year;
- target for number of new customers;
- target for number of retained customers;
- expected year the practice will become cash-flow positive;
- anticipated revenue for first two years;
- anticipated revenue by year five.

Market for the Consultancy: Like an attorney making his case in front of a jury, you need to justify to yourself why your product/service is needed. There are two great sources where you can find marketing information: www.ceoexpress.com and www.cyberatlas.com. These Web sites contain research from all of the top market research firms (two to three pages in length).

Sales: A detailed description of who you plan to sell your services to and what tactics you will use to sell the services. For example, the targeted user might be a company president and the tactics to be used might be direct mail, trade shows, and seminars (one to two pages in length).

Marketing Strategy: A detailed description of how the consultancy plans to develop a recognizable name through the use of various marketing tools such as direct mail, public relations, speaking at seminars, print advertising, banner advertising, and so on (one to two pages in length).

Revenue: A description of each source of revenue (one to two pages in length).

Retention Plan: The hardest part of building a business is trying to retain your customers. Too many entrepreneurs focus on the initial sale and not on how they plan to support new customers once they have committed. Getting new customers is a lot more difficult and financially costly than retaining existing customers (one to two pages in length).

*M*any consultants don't bother to prepare this section because they think only about the per-hour charge they will bill for their services. The purpose of this section is to think about both your consulting fees and what other services you can offer to drive revenue. My own business plan helped me come up with the idea of starting a service to help my clients obtain speaking engagements to raise their visibility to attract new business. That realization laid the foundation for www.freeSpeakers.org, which helps business professionals use speaking as a marketing tool. Now we have 100 corporate clients.

Competition: The worst mistake consultants can make in developing their business plan is to say that they don't have any competition. Everyone has competition, whether it is direct or indirect. You need to perform a strengths and weaknesses analysis on each competitor. I typically paste the competition's home page on top of the analysis. A chart showing the differences between your consultancy and the competition will make your case for funding stronger (three to five pages in length).

Advisory Board: Being a consultant can be a lonely business. Developing an advisory board of clients and non-competitive successful consultants will give you people to bounce ideas off of and challenge your assumptions. A one-paragraph description of what type of people you are looking for and a prospective list of candidates would focus your thinking on appropriate advisors. A startup consulting practice doesn't need more than five advisors (one page in length).

Operations Plan: A description of how you plan to support your marketing, sales, and client-retention efforts. For example, I am big on sending out books and publication articles on a variety of topics to my clients. This is time-consuming, but worthwhile because it shows the client that I am thinking about them and that I am taking the time to understand their business. I realized that for me to do this effectively I needed someone to send out certain well-chosen publications, so I asked my wife to handle this function. This section should also cover administration, technology, Web development, and accounting (one to two pages in length).

Launch Plan: A spreadsheet detailing what you plan to do in each of the consultancy's first 12 months of existence.

This would cover the number of prospects visited, publications to contact, number of prospects converted into clients, and so forth (one to two pages).

Financials: One-year financial and one-year cash-flow projections. You don't need an accountant to do this for you. If you know how to operate an Excel spreadsheet you can do it yourself. Accountants are a waste of money for you at this time because they would rely on you to tell them your revenue forecasts and to list and explain each of your expense categories. Provide notes detailing the calculations you used to build your forecasts at the end of the financials. Have an accountant review the financials to make sure all of the formulas are accurate. Nothing is more embarrassing than numbers that don't add up correctly (three to five pages in length).

No two businesses or business plans are alike because the market you may be going after or serving is different from someone else's in another geographic area. Nonetheless, most plans follow a well-tried and tested structure, and general advice on preparing a plan is universally applicable.

Sample Business Plan

What follows is the plan I used to start my business. Every summer I review this plan while I am sitting on the beach in Ocean City, New Jersey, and decide what I have done right and what needs to be changed.

Kramer Communications Business Plan

Mission

To provide business planning, development, and marketing services to small- and medium-size companies from Philadelphia to New York.

Service Description

Kramer Communications provides three types of services, all focused on new business generation and client retention:

Plan Development and Execution

- **Business Plan**—The business plans we develop are focused on helping business owners tell an exciting story that will attract institutional, corporate, and/or private venture capital.
- **Marketing Plan**—We develop marketing plans that focus on the least expensive ways of building visibility and obtaining face time with potential clients.
- **Sales Plan**—We co-develop sales plans with the presidents and vice presidents of sales. Our business plans walk the reader through the sales process that our clients go through or should go through. We then write about which industries the client does, should, or will focus on and the job titles of the target contacts in those companies. Once this is done, we develop one-year forecasts.
- **Hiring Plan**—We work with management to develop plans for hiring new employees over specified periods of time. We develop the job descriptions and profiles of the type of people our clients want to hire, and lists of organizations, colleges, and other resources to contact to attract those individuals.
- **Client Retention**—We interview our clients' customers by telephone and ask them a variety of questions related to our client's existing products and services, employees, and new products and services our client should consider offering. Then we make recommendations based on our findings and review them with our clients.
- **Employee Retention**—We interview our client's employees to find out what they think of the company as a whole, management, and ask for suggestions they may have to improve the company and what new products and services the company should be offering.

- **Expert Witness**—We provide expert-witness planning and testimony for law firms in trials related to e-commerce.

Business Development Services

- **Prospect Surveys**—We interview our client's prospects and ask what they plan to spend their capital budget on over the next year, how they view our client, and whether they would consider buying from our client.
- **Seminar Development and Execution**—We create seminar ideas or take our clients' ideas and develop a plan to execute those seminars. The seminar plans include targeted companies and titles of individuals within those companies, and the number of prospective attendees to invite to the seminars.

Capital Raising

- **Business Plan Evaluations**—We review and critique each section of a client's business plan and provide suggestions on how to improve the plan in order to make it more appealing to potential investors.
- **Investor Identification**—We develop a list of potential institutional, corporate, and individual investors who would have an interest in reviewing our client's business plan.
- **Investor Marketing**—We develop both e-mail and print letters to be sent to prospective investors identified by Kramer Communications or those whom the client has identified. These letters are usually four to five paragraphs long and focus on the market need for the client's product or service, the client's target industry, the client's experience, and an estimate of the cost of the client's services.
- **Providing Investor Questions**—We develop a list of 60 to 70 questions that investors are most likely to ask our clients. Clients are asked to cut and paste the answers to the questions from their business plans. Any questions that can't be answered must be addressed in the plan.
- **Client Presentation**—We assist clients in developing presentations for potential investors, both in print and Microsoft PowerPoint. We assist in writing, rewriting, and reviewing presentation material developed by the client.

Competitive Advantages

There are a handful of independent consultants in the Philadelphia–New York region who write various types of business-related plans. Most of these individuals are former accountants, bank loan officers, and economic development professionals. Kramer Communications is superior to competitors for the following reasons:

- **Business Launch and Operational Experience**—We have launched and run businesses as diverse as e-commerce sites, direct marketing, magazines, newspapers, Internet development, trade associations, and business incubators.
- **Business Financing Expertise**—We have experience in assisting our clients in raising capital from private, institutional, and corporate venture capitalists. We have assisted our clients in raising as little as $100,000 and as much as $3 million through investment contacts and assistance in structuring deals.
- **High-Level Business Contacts**—We have developed a database of more than 3,000 high-level global executive contacts. We connect our clients with our contacts to create new business opportunities for clients.
- **Technology Expertise**—We have built and run global computer and telecommunication systems and e-commerce sites.
- **Turnaround Expertise**—We have turned around a mall, magazine, information systems department, multimedia development company, and trade association. The turnarounds we have worked with have ranged in size from a few employees to 50 employees and $3 million in sales.
- **Willingness to Take Equity**—No matter what the economic climate, we are willing to take a third of our compensation in equity from any client to back up our work.

Target Market

There are three groups Kramer Communications needs to build visibility and credibility with.

Influencers

- Accountants
- Commercial Bankers
- Corporate Attorneys
- Investment Bankers
- Patent Attorneys

- Venture Capitalists

Industry Targets

- Advertising/Marketing Firms
- Financial Institutions
- E-Commerce
- Information Systems
- Money Management
- Software

Buyer Targets at Industry Firms

- President
- Vice President of Sales
- Vice President of Marketing
- Director of Marketing

Marketing

There are seven tools we use to increase visibility.

1. **Authoring Books:** Authoring books increases our visibility in the business community, and gives us access to professionals who can refer businesses to us, retain us for work with their companies, and become strategic partners. We have developed four books in the last five years and are preparing to develop a fifth book.

2. **Clipping Service:** In order to show our clients and prospects we are thinking of them and that we take the time to understand their issues, we have and will send articles related to their industry.

3. **Organization Sponsorship:** We have sponsored and joined the boards and subcommittees of such organizations as the Entrepreneur's Forum of Greater Philadelphia and the Chester County Chamber of Commerce. Below is a list of organizations we need to consider joining and becoming more involved in:

   - Digital Delaware
   - Greater Philadelphia Venture Group
   - Greater Philadelphia Chamber of Commerce
   - Great Valley Chamber of Commerce
   - New York New Media Group

- New Jersey Technology Council

4. **Speaking at Conferences and Seminars:** We have spoken at a few local seminars and conferences run by the Entrepreneur's Forum of Greater Philadelphia, the Technology Resource Alliance, and trade association meetings for accountants and money managers. We need to speak in front of organizations such as the following:

- American Management Association
- Greater Philadelphia Venture Group
- New Jersey Technology Council

5. **Strategic Partnerships:** We don't have any strategic partnerships at this time. Appropriate strategic partners would be accounting, banking, investment banking, and law firms interested in the development and implementation that we currently offer. Organizations that might be a good fit would be as follows:

Accounting

- Gocial and Company
- Goldenberg Rosenthal
- Grant Thornton
- Joseph P. Melvin Company
- Smart & Associates

Banking

- Commerce Bank
- Commonwealth Bank
- Downingtown National Bank
- First Financial Bank
- Progress Bank
- Silicon Valley Bank
- Sovereign Bank
- First National Bank of Chester County

Law

- Blank Rome
- Bramson & Pressman
- Cozen & O'Connor
- Duane Morris Hecksher

- Klehr Harrison
- Morgan Lewis & Bockius
- Morrison Forester
- Reed Smith
- Schnader Harrison
- Stradley Ronon
- Wolf Block

Investment Banks

- Berkshire Capital
- Broadview Associates
- Hamilton Capital
- Janney Montgomery Scott
- Promark
- Tower Hill Capital

6. **Web Site:** We have developed a Web site that tells who we are and what we do. It also provides insights into how to market a company and sells our books. In addition, however, we need to give examples of how we have made a difference with our clients and to develop other sources of information so clients and prospects will want to bookmark our site. For example, we should have links to capital-raising sources, organizations to join, and trade associations that reflect our clients' interests.

7. **Writing Columns:** We currently write for one regional newspaper. We need to expand the number of newspapers we write for in order to increase potential deal flow. In order to do this, we need to put together a list of publications targeted by geographic area and send out a package of sample articles for editors to review. We can offer our columns for free for three months and then talk to the editor about paying for them.

Sales

Kramer Communications gets new clients by doing the following:

Prospecting Process

- **Client Referrals:** We will speak with clients about potential opportunities with other clients. Clients who refer new business will be offered either a 10 percent finder's fee or an equal amount as a reduction in their bill, as a way of saying thank you for the business.

- **Events:** Kramer Communications has met new clients at events. The organizations where we have made the best contacts are the Greater Philadelphia Venture Group, Entrepreneurs Forum of Greater Philadelphia, Chester County Chamber of Commerce, and the New York New Media Group.
- **Influencer Meetings:** Ninety percent of Kramer Communications' current business comes from referrals from accounting, commercial bank, law, investment bank, and venture capitalists.
- **Nonclient Referrals:** Kramer Communications has received client referrals from friends and nonclient business associates. Kramer Communications needs to spend more time educating these groups in order to generate more referrals.
- **Writing Leads:** Marc Kramer writes a weekly business column for the *Times-Herald* of Norristown, Pennsylvania, part of the Journal Register, a national newspaper chain. On average, one reader a month calls Kramer Communications asking about engaging his services.

Prospecting Follow-Up

Step One: Send an e-mail letter to every person we met at an event within 48 hours of meeting them. The e-mail contains mention of where we met, what Kramer Communications does, and our interest in meeting the influencer or prospect to better understand his or her business.

Step Two: Call the influencer or prospect to see if we can set up a breakfast or lunch meeting.

Step Three: Determine after meeting whether the prospect or influencer can provide potential business and what Kramer Communications can do for that prospect.

Revenue Sources

Current Sources of Revenue

- **Writing Books:** For the last four years, Marc Kramer has landed one new book contract per year. He has also developed proposals for three other books and is shopping those proposals around. The average contract has been $10,000 per book, plus 10 percent of the retail price.
- **Business Referrals:** Kramer Communications has agreements with ten companies to receive a finder's fee of between 5 and 10 percent for any new business referred by Kramer Communications to strategic partners. Kramer Communications is only paid when the strategic partner is paid.

- **Capital Finder's Fees:** Kramer Communications assists companies in getting their business plans in front of potential investors. For assisting companies in raising capital, Kramer Communications receives a nonrefundable retainer of $5,000 plus the Lehman Formula (5 percent of the first million, 4 percent of the second million, 3 percent of the third million, 2 percent of the fourth million, and 1 percent beyond four million).
- **Outsource Management:** Kramer Communications has supported clients in a variety of management roles such as Chief Executive Officer, Chief Operating Officer, Chief Marketing Officer, Director of Marketing, and Director of New Ventures. The fees for fulfilling these rolls have ranged from $2,000 to $4,000 a month.
- **Newspaper Columns:** Marc Kramer writes business columns for two newspapers: the Eastern Business Journal and the Times-Herald.
- **Plan Development:** Kramer Communications develops business, sales, operating, marketing, e-commerce, and customer retention plans. The fees for these plans range from $5,000 to $15,000. The average fee is $10,000.

Potential Sources of Revenue

- **Business Turnaround:** Kramer Communications has not leveraged its experience and expertise in turning around businesses.
- **On-line Book Evaluation:** Kramer Communications has developed an expertise in what it takes to obtain a book contract. We understand how to develop a successful proposal and a successful query letter, how to select an agent, and how to develop new proposal opportunities. We will develop and evaluate a plan to provide on-line assistance to those whose dream it is to obtain book contracts. Initially, we will focus on business books.
- **On-line Business Plan Development:** Kramer Communications will develop an on-line service for aspiring entrepreneurs that allows them to develop a business plan on-line and then e-mail that plan to prospective investors.
- **Syndicated Columns:** Kramer Communications will investigate hiring a college student to market Marc Kramer's business columns to daily and weekly newspapers.

Client Retention

Current Retention Tools

- **Books:** At least once a year, we will send a book to clients that will influence or enhance their thinking about their industry, new sales and marketing techniques, and leadership.

- **Christmas Gifts:** Each Christmas, we will send a tin of TastyKakes, which are made in Philadelphia, to our clients. We will reevaluate sending tins at Christmas and send them instead on the anniversary of Marc Kramer's starting Kramer Communications.

- **Client New Business:** We will make a list of all our clients to see which clients could be matched up for new business opportunities. Kramer Communications will evaluate each new business contact made and determine if that contact could be a potential client for existing and new clients.

- **Event Tickets:** Kramer Communications will provide free sports and theater tickets to clients as a way of saying thank-you for their business.

- **Newspaper Articles:** Kramer Communications will send copies of articles to clients that pertain to the client's business, or suggest new sales, marketing, technology, and capital-raising ideas.

- **Round Table:** We will offer current and past clients the opportunity to get together to speak about different topics related to business.

- **Seminar:** We will run a once-a-year seminar featuring clients as speakers. The seminars will focus on building sales, creating greater visibility, raising capital, employee retention, and employee recruitment.

- **Social Event:** We will consider having a cookout each summer and inviting past and present clients. This will allow Kramer Communications to socialize with clients in a nonbusiness environment.

Financials

Income

Plan Development	$70,000
Outsourced Chief Marketing Officer	72,000
Outsourced CEO	96,000
Writing	15,000
Total	**$253,000**

Expenses

Outside Contractor	36,000
Federal Taxes	40,000
State Taxes	6,000

Local Taxes	2,000
Health Insurance	12,000
Car Insurance	1,400
Life Insurance	2,200
Car Gas	2,400
Supplies	5,000
Electric	2,400
Inside Telephone	1,400
Mobile Telephone	1,100
Entertainment	2,100
Travel	1,100
Internet Connection	400
Postage	600
Memberships	1,500
Retirement	4,000
Charity	4,000
Total	**81,600**
Profit/Loss	**$171,400**

Interview with a Sales Consultant

Elliot Levine is the founder and managing partner of The Sales Factory, a sales consulting company, which develops turnkey sales models for businesses. Services range from developing "go to market" strategies, organizational structures and compensation plans, to flow-charting and scripting sales processes. Prior to founding The Sales Factory, Mr. Levine was president and CEO of Savoir Technology, a leading supplier of mid-range UNIX-based systems, both branded (IBM, NCR, Unisys) and white box. Mr. Levine oversaw the company's three divisions: VAR System Sales, Storage, and OEM Assembly, which built a wide variety of custom systems for companies in the telecom, entertainment, and mail services industries. Savoir was sold to Avnet Computer in 1999.

Before joining Savoir, Mr. Levine spent four years as president and COO of Softmart, Inc., a global reseller of computer products and services. Prior to his arrival, Softmart was a software-only reseller servicing the Fortune 500 marketplace. During his tenure Mr. Levine started the company's small business division and also moved the company into the hardware arena, gaining authorization from key vendors such as HP, IBM, and Compaq. Mr. Levine also served for four years on Microsoft's Reseller Executive Council.

Mr. Levine has held a variety of other executive sales and marketing positions throughout his career including Vice President and General Manager of ENSONIQ's multimedia division, and Vice President of Sales for Merisel, Inc., a global provider of PC hardware and software, where he managed three of the company's five divisions and a $1.7 billion sales budget.

Mr. Levine graduated magna cum laude from the University of Massachusetts.

Question: Why did you become a consultant?

Response: I had moved many times in my career and I decided based on my family. As my children got older they didn't want to move anymore. I didn't want to be a victim of a company being merged or acquired or downsized. I wanted control over my life.

Question: How much money did it take to start your consulting practice?

Response: About $1,000.

Question: Did you write a business plan for yourself?

Response: Not at first. In the beginning there was low-hanging fruit from former employers and friends and family. I developed a plan about 18 months after I got into it. I think it is worthwhile and it doesn't need to be robust. The important part of the plan is getting clients. It's establishing a specific niche or expertise.

Question: How long have you been a consultant?

Response: Three years.

Question: What is the best part of being a consultant?

Response: There is usually a pressing need for the actions and activities you engage in. When you work for someone you can be in a maintenance mode for months. In consulting there is a pressing need, and you are brought in to make an effective change.

Question: What is the worst part of being a consultant?

Response: There isn't a lot of camaraderie and you are constantly prospecting.

Question: What is the hardest part of being a consultant?

Response: Getting clients is the most difficult part. In my practice I have to create the need and provide a solution and the sales cycle is long. There are a variety of problems such as people changes, budget changes, the company gets acquired, etc. The cycle can last three to six months or even more.

Question: What do you like best about what you do?

Response: I find it gratifying to create a business from nothing. It's nice to build something from nothing. There are no hidden cameras or names to hide behind. It all depends on your guile and smarts.

Question: What do you like least about what you do?

Response: The uncertainty and not being able to take a deep breath and relax.

Question: How did you figure what to charge your clients?

Response: I felt my way in the dark. There are formulas and rates for what people charge. My projects are usually long-term. Companies don't want to pay an hourly rate. I look at what the customer can afford. I charge what the market will bear. Sometimes I look at it as a strategic investment.

Question: How did you get your first client?

Response: I called people I knew in the industry. I said, "If you have any projects and it's taking longer than it should, then maybe I can help." I got my largest contract that way.

Question: How do you market and sell yourself?

Response: I think networking is a great way to get business. I have been focusing on VCs and marketing through e-mails and phone calls. It's smiling and dialing and doing follow-up e-mails and calls.

Question: How much experience do you think someone needs before he or she can go out and become a consultant?

Response: Probably more than they think. I think you need at least ten years of experience to prove you can add value. I ask people why they agreed to see me and they tell me it is because I ran two companies. Titles you have had, your expertise and the companies you have worked for all play a part.

Question: How long did it take you until you were making the same salary and benefits you had when you were employed by someone else?

Response: I am still not there yet. I was doing very well. It will probably take another couple of years.

Question: Did your spouse work to support you as you grew your consulting practice?

Response: No!

Question: Do you ask for a retainer before you do your work and, if so, how much?

Response: I look for 50 percent up front.

Question: Have you ever had a client that refused to pay and, if so, what did you do?

Response: No!

Question: What's the one piece of advice you would give a new consultant?

Response: Make sure you have the time to make it successful. I am talking about having enough money in the bank.

Chapter Summary

Developing a business plan is absolutely essential regardless of whether you are trying to raise money or not. You need a business plan to see what flaws your business model may have and to communicate a clear vision and direction for your employees, board members, and potential investors.

Chapter Key Points

- The most important and difficult sections to prepare relate to marketing and sales, as these can make or break not only the business plan but also the business itself!

- When putting together financial projections, create a one-year forecast and a one-year cash-flow statement. Planning more than a year in advance is a waste of time because of the rapid changes in today's economy. Microsoft Office comes with financial spreadsheets and financial modeling options. Two other good software packages designed to assist with business plan writing are Plan A (from Internet Capital Bulletin Board, Inc.) and Plan Write (from

Business Resource Software, Inc.). Both packages ask the user a series of questions, which the user types in. When the user finishes answering all of the questions, a formal business plan with financials is provided.

 When drafting the plan, be positive but realistic about the business's prospects, and explicitly recognize and respond honestly to shortcomings and risks.

Avoid unnecessary jargon, economize on words, and use short, crisp sentences and bullet points. Always check to make sure all words are spelled correctly. If you decide to show outsiders, you want to demonstrate that you are a professional. When there are significant issues, break the text into numbered paragraphs or sections and relegate detail to appendices.

Get a qualified outsider to review your plan in draft form. Be prepared to adjust the plan in light of the reviewer's comment.

Support market and sales projections with market research. Ensure that there is a direct relationship between market analysis, sales forecasts, and financial projections. Assess competitors' positions and possible responses realistically.

Restrict the level of detail on product specifications and technical issues.

Be realistic about sales expectations, profit margins, and funding requirements. Ensure that financial ratios are in line with industry norms. Do not underestimate the cost and time required for marketing yourself and setting up your office. Consider the possibility of the halve-double rule: halve the sales projections and double the cost and time required.

DEVELOPING A COMPANY NAME

CREATING YOUR IDENTITY ◀

O*ne of the first big challenges you will face when starting a consulting practice is figuring out what to name your company. Many people believe that picking the right name will make a significant difference in whether they succeed or fail. They believe the right name will create "buzz" and the wrong name will make it difficult for people to remember them.*

Large corporations that are going through a name change or naming a new division will hire marketing firms that specialize in developing names. One of my clients spent over $100,000 researching names and testing them on prospective buyers. I believe that choosing a bad name can damage or kill a business, but spending a lot of money on developing a name is not significantly better than simply making a list and selecting one that you and your advisors, friends, and potential clients find to be acceptable. No matter what your name is, you still need to deliver results.

Before you put pen to paper or strike a key in your quest to find the appropriate name, keep in mind the following:

- **Audience:** Many companies have made mistakes by picking names that are culturally offensive. The last thing you want to do is to insult an ethnic group.
- **Length of Name:** Make sure the name is easy to spell. You don't want someone going to an Internet search engine or calling information and misspelling your name because it is either too long or so unusual that they can't get it right.
- **Meaning:** Pick words that convey a positive image.
- **Service:** Think about words that best describe your service. You don't want to pick words with meanings that have little to do with your service or that will confuse potential clients.

Name Origins

Most consultants don't have any scientific process for developing a name or can't afford to hire a marketing research firm to develop a name. Most names of companies come from the following 15 origins:

Animals: Some people choose names of animals, such as tigers (www.tigerconsulting.com, a software-consulting firm in Thailand), to show that they are aggressive and hard-driving.

Child's Name: Many people have used their children's first names in order to honor their children.

City: I don't think there is a city in America whose name hasn't been used in the name of a consulting firm. People use city names because it makes them seem bigger than they are, the name of the city is easily memorable, or the name of the city will show up higher on Internet searches.

*I*n the last chapter, I mentioned a service my wife and I started called freeSpeakers (www.freespeakers.org) and the name tells the user everything. Our speakers are willing to speak for free, which encourages many business-focused nonprofits to use our service for finding quality speakers.

County: Consultants who focus on a specific county use the name of the county for the same reasons people choose cities.

Country: The reason a consultant chooses a country is to convey a sense of reach and because the name is usually memorable.

Descriptive: Using a descriptive word tells people what you do. Elliot Levin, who is interviewed in this book about how to build sales, calls his company Sales Factor, and Francine Carb, who is also interviewed, named her company Markitects.

Full Names: The most famous full name I can think of is JP Morgan, the bank named for the investment banker, that is now part of JP Morgan Chase & Company, a combination investment and commercial bank.

Home or Business Address: Some people use their street addresses as their business name. There is a marketing firm in New York called Broadway Associates. *The Wall Street Journal* named itself after the street they were on so they would be easily memorable to the stock traders and investment bankers who populated Wall Street.

Last Names: Use your name if it is well known so that when you walk into a room or speak with people, they can identify you easily. I use my last name in my consulting practice because I ran a large trade association in my region and have served on many regional boards.

Mythological: There is a German information systems consulting firm that named itself after the Greek god Zeus. Using a mythological name connotes certain meanings to knowledgeable individuals.

Plants: People will select plants to convey a certain image, for example, certain types of trees and plants such as cactus, maples, sunflower, roses, and so on. A commercial real estate company in Chicago is called The Rose Group (www.therosegroup.com). The idea of smelling like a rose is one that appeals to a lot of companies.

Service/Product Names: A client of mine used the name of the software he developed, ReviewNet (www.reviewnet.com), which evaluates information technology professionals' skill levels, as his company name in order to boost the name of the company. One of my ventures is called Bizlaunch (www.bizlaunch.net) and the name tells you that the service helps people start businesses.

Parent's Names: I have known people who chose a parent's name to honor that parent.

Rich-Sounding/Historical Names: Some people like names because they sound upper class, sophisticated, or they are connected with a dead president, such as Rockefeller, Lincoln, Washington, or Jefferson.

Unusual Names: A friend of mine chose the name Antiphony (www.antiphony.com) for his consulting practice. The unusual name triggered a call from me to ask him what he does. The downside of an unusual name is that sometimes it's hard for people to remember or they can't mentally file it.

Expert Advice

I interviewed Francine Carb, founder and CEO of Markitects, Inc., a strategic marketing communications firm that creates unique solutions to support branding, positioning, and launching of technology companies. Since 1994, the company has launched 65 technology products

Some of the greatest business leaders, such as Disney, Ford, and Trump, all used their last names. Be careful if your name is long and unwieldy. You don't want prospective customers to become frustrated because they can't spell your name and therefore can't find you by telephone or through the Internet.

and services. She also serves on the Board of Directors for the Monument Group, a series of mutual funds in Washington, D.C., and the Board of Advisors for The Technology Resource Alliance, a consortium of business and financial professionals. She is also involved in the National Association of Women Business Owners (NAWBO) and The Forum of Executive Women. Francine has a B.A. in Economics from Lafayette College and an M.B.A. in Marketing from St. Joseph's University.

Question: How should a new company go about selecting a name?

Response: If it is a small consulting firm made up of one person or group of partners, there are two avenues to go down. You can take your last name. The other path is to do what large companies do and that is look at the market the company is serving, the characteristics of the buyer, and the competitors in that field. Then embark on a creative brainstorming process.

Question: What type of research do you do when developing a name for a client's business?

Response: The first thing we do is break down the market, the customer's characteristics, and the competition. We look at the common words used in that market segment. When looking at customer characteristics, we look at the benefits the customer will receive. In the case of competitors we are interested in the names that competitors are using. For example, in the financial industry, are the competitors using the words *bond* or *trust* in their names? I suggest that, if you are going to use a name other than your own, you should go down all three avenues.

Question: What are the pluses and minuses of using your last name?

Response: The pluses are if you have a reputation in your field of expertise then you have a brand. If you don't have a well-known name and want to create a name in the field, that will help create a brand.

The down side of using your last name is that people will assume you are a one-person company and that will have limitations. You have to decide whether you are going to grow a business or stay a one-person consulting firm.

Another down side is that when you sell your business your company may not have as high a valuation because people associate the business with the founder if his or her name is on the door. The founder who uses his name is the brand and that can be problematic because you are the brand.

Question: What are the pluses and minuses of creating a name that isn't your last name?

Response: The pluses are that you have an unlimited creative palette. You can build a name, brand, and meaning to the markets you are serving. It implicitly makes the statement you are an organization as opposed to an individual. The third advantage is in attracting employees. Employees typically like to work for a firm or company as opposed to the perception that the company is smaller because the person has used his or her last name. Buyers believe the company is bigger because of the last name being different than the owners' and the buyer will think you have more capabilities.

Question: Should you run the various names you are considering past clients and prospects before selecting a name?

Response: Yes! I suggest doing it formally or informally. You should do a focus study. The reason to do it is to weed out negative connotations or associations. Don't open it up to customers by asking them what name you should use. If you are going to ask your customer what he or she thinks, narrow your choices to three and present them to customers.

Question: Should you have an attorney or a marketing firm determine if the name is being used?

Response: The best way to find out whether a name is being used is to go to the U.S. Trademarks Web site and see what names or phrases are being used. You can go to a dot.com registration site and see if your name is taken. Chances are that whatever name you have selected is taken. You can still use a name already taken if you are using it for a different industry. You may not be able to trademark the name, but you may be able to use it anyway. If you want to trademark it then you have to go to an intellectual property attorney. Few names are ever trademarked because it is so difficult. If you are going to build a big company then you might consider it.

Question: How much should someone budget to research and develop a list of potential names for a small startup business?

Response: A minimal amount of money to do this correctly is probably around $10,000. It takes about four weeks to do.

Question: Do you need to consider what that name will mean when translated into different languages?

Response: If you are marketing outside the United States or thinking of marketing outside the United States, then the answer is yes. If you are primarily marketing in the United States, the answer is no.

Question: What is the one mistake you have seen businesses make when selecting a name?

Response: One mistake I have seen is they go through a methodical procedure and then they go to a family member and decide to use that person's choice. Unfortunately, the family member more than likely can't make an informed decision. Another mistake is picking a name similar to a competitor's. If you like your competitor's name, admire it, but don't steal it.

Question: What is the one piece of advice you would give when creating a name?

Response: You should take it seriously and not just blow it off. It is going to be your identity, hopefully, for a long time to come.

Chapter Key Points

🔑 Don't spend an enormous amount of time on it and don't get too cute. When developing a name, ask yourself the following questions:

- What is the image you want to project?
- What words could your intended audience find offensive?
- Do you want a name that describes your product?
- Do you want to build brand recognition for your own name?
- Is your name well known enough that it would attract business?

🔑 I am partial either to using last names or names that describe what the consultancy does.

🔑 Taking a risk with a name that people find hard to remember, or with one that may be open to ridicule, or with one that leaves people scratching their heads, could significantly decrease your chances of success.

🔑 A poor name choice makes a statement about you professionally.

🔑 Take your time, but don't make a crusade out of it that ends in frustration or holds you up from moving the business forward.

SEEKING PROFESSIONAL ADVISORS

Most people who get into consulting don't think of themselves as a business. They don't realize and appreciate that they need the same type of professional support their clients do. You need to think of yourself as a world-class company and hire the best advisors. Good advisors bring both the knowledge of their profession and business contacts that can lead to new opportunities.

Selecting good outside professionals can be a time-consuming job, but it's well worth the investment. Questions to ask when hiring outside professionals include:

1. Do they understand my business?
2. How many years have they been in the business?
3. Have they ever worked with a startup consultancy?
4. Are their fees reasonable?
5. Will they work with me financially if I can't afford their full fees in the beginning?
6. What do their clients say about them?
7. When clients have left them, what were the reasons?
8. Will they invite me to events they sponsor even though I am a sole practitioner?
9. Will a seasoned executive be assigned to me or will we be used to allow a junior executive to obtain some experience?

10. Will they introduce us to their other clients who might bring us business?

Accountants, Bankers, and Lawyers

Most people take a friend's referral, call someone on the basis of an advertisement, or hire someone they met at an event. Selecting someone that a trusted business associate met through a referral or event is a good way to get started, but should not be the full extent of a service-provider search. Selecting the wrong type of outside professionals can cost you just as much money as underestimating the cost of a project.

You need to be selective and thorough in your evaluation and choice of key outside professionals. Most companies need four types of professionals: an accountant, a banker, an insurance broker, and a lawyer. Let's discuss each of the questions that open this chapter and how they relate to hiring outside professionals.

1. Do they understand my business? All too often, business people hire outside professionals based on personality or a friend's recommendation. They hire an accountant because they hear she is meticulous and got a tax refund for a friend. A friend said this lawyer was terrific with the incorporation process. The insurance broker got a lower premium on someone else's professional liability insurance. The banker helped a friend get an increased line of credit.

Such references are a good start, but what you really need to know is whether the professional can handle the needs of a consulting practice.

- **Accountant:** You need an accountant who is familiar with the tax issues and costs related to a service business.

> *My accounting firm told me that I could deduct all of my health insurance premiums if I put my wife on the payroll and paid for her health insurance. That piece of advice saved me $4,000, triple the amount I paid them to do my taxes.*

The Banker Is My Friend

A fellow consultant, who ran an advertising/marketing practice, wanted to develop a Web site that would allow her customers to download various types of sample presentations, brochures, and business cards. The service was going to be tied into a monthly retainer fee. The amount of money she needed to build the site exceeded her line of credit. Because the banker had spent enough time with my business associate and knew many of her customers, she was able to make a strong case to the loan committee to increase her line of credit.

- **Banker:** You want a banker who has loaned money to startup consulting practices, has set up lines of credit, and is an advocate on your behalf with the loan committee.

I interviewed Frank Masterangelo, President/Chief Operating Officer of The Bancorp, on how a consultant should go about selecting a banker. He is the former Senior Vice President, Chief Technology Officer, and Co-Chair of the Technology Committee for the former Jefferson Bank, now Hudson Valley Bank, which he joined in 1995. Frank created and had full oversight for the Information Systems Group, including Network Management, End User Support, Disaster Recovery, Applications Development, Database Administration, End User Training, and Voice Systems. In 1997, Frank was named Jefferson's Officer of the Year. Frank has a B.S. in accounting from St. Joseph's University in Philadelphia.

Question: What criteria should a person use to evaluate banks?

Response: There are a number of things, for example, the scope of products available such as interest rates on deposits and commercial loan rates. You should try to talk to other customers of the banks and speak to other small

> *A client of mine needed a $1 million line of credit to expand his business. His current bank was one of the largest in the nation and, over the three years he had been a customer, they had changed the bank officer he dealt with three times. When he wanted to expand his line from $250,000, the loan officer who had inherited his account knew nothing about his business and viewed my client as just another loan. My client changed to a smaller bank with less loan officer turnover that understood his business.*

businesses and inquire about the level of service you can expect. Make sure the service levels are acceptable to you.

Question: Should you try to develop a relationship with one person in the bank?

Response: It makes sense to develop a relationship with one person who understands your business and your needs. In my opinion, it is better to have a relationship with one officer rather than trying to get to know people in each department.

Question: What type of an account should a new business open?

Response: It depends on the type of business and the amount of activity you expect for the account. At the very least you will need a commercial transaction account. If your business has employees you will also need a payroll account. If you have some cash float, you might consider a money market account.

Question: Should a new business apply for a line of credit when starting?

Response: It depends what the business has as collateral. It is advisable to attain one as soon as possible. No matter how small your business is, you can get a line of credit as long as you are willing to guarantee it.

Question: How much of a line of credit should a person apply for?

Response: Anyone who is starting a consulting business should apply for at least 60 to 90 days worth of cash flow. This will allow sufficient time to collect money that is owed and still run the business until the checks come in.

Question: What value-added services outside of bank services should one look for when selecting a bank?

Response: There are a handful of things. The better the bank understands the customer's industry the better for the company, for example, what assets of the business are being pledged for credit? Access to decision makers in the bank is also important. The last thing a customer wants is to deal with a lot of red tape. Another factor to consider is whether the bank networks for its customers and helps them grow. You might also look for a bank that can handle your company's payroll service or bring in other trusted value-added providers.

Question: What's the value of using Internet banking?

Response: There are a variety of reasons. You have access to all of the detailed information that you would only receive on your monthly statement and you can get it 24/7. You can transact business when you want to. You can download account information into almost any accounting software that you may be running. The advantages are about convenience for the business. You can access the information anywhere you have an Internet connection.

Question: What is the one mistake businesspeople make when selecting a bank for business?

Response: They make the decision solely on interest rate alone or the interest on the deposit account, or they continue to bank where they have always banked and haven't looked for a bank that would be the best fit for their business.

2. How many years have they been in the business? Experience is very important to any business, but it could mean the difference between success and failure for a new company. You want professionals who have been around long enough to have personally experienced the unavoidable ups and downs of business. You should look at professionals with 10 to 15 years of experience because these people have gone through ups and downs and have learned most of the tricks of their trade.

- **Accountant:** An experienced accountant will know what hidden expenses to look for that can be eliminated or provide additional deductions. Someone who has been around for a while lends credibility when going to a bank for a line of credit.
- **Banker:** Experienced loan officers know how to fight for their customers to get an extension or additional capital. They know how to best structure debt for it to be acceptable to the bank without, at the same time, putting their customer out of business.
- **Lawyer:** Be careful about using inexperienced lawyers. When lawyers first graduate from law school, they take up defensive postures that are meant to protect the client. They aren't yet problem solvers and they don't necessarily know how to put business deals together. Inexperienced lawyers can be deal killers. You need attorneys who are experienced in contract law, who know how to make an agreement that protects you without forcing your prospective client to send it to their lawyer for review and possible changes. The contract should be written in simple enough terms that no further legal expertise is required.

3. Has the individual ever worked with a startup consultancy? I work with a lot of startup companies and I understand their needs for expediency and reduced fees. There are, however, many consultants who are used to dealing with large companies and have a difficult time dealing with startups. The same issues crop up when selecting professional advisors. You need advisors who understand that you are on a limited budget, you need to move quickly, and

> *In the Philadelphia area, there was an accountant named Howard Ross, who was a partner at one of the national accounting firms. Howard struck fear into the hearts of his competitors because there were few times he lost when companies were considering whether to use him or another firm. Why was Howard so successful? As one of my clients told me, "he took the time to understand my business."*

Get Lawyers Who Know Their Stuff

A friend who provided computer project management consulting had an opportunity to do a large consulting project for a *Fortune* 1000 company. He knew many lawyers who could do an adequate job to keep him out of trouble, but he only knew a couple of attorneys who knew how to structure and quickly close a deal. He selected a lawyer who had 20 years of experience dealing with long-term consulting contracts with large companies. The lawyer's acumen in this area saved my friend a lot of time and money and, more importantly, protected my friend from being liable for events that weren't directly related to his work.

you need advice that matches your budget.

- **Accountant:** A good accountant will be able to help you set up your own books on your computer or recommend or provide an inexpensive bookkeeper to handle your financial records. A good accountant will also provide you with a list of do's and don'ts and reminders about what you can and should deduct and what you can't deduct.

- **Banker:** You don't want a banker who immediately pulls the company's line of credit because you are having a bad quarter and are having difficulty making loan payments. You should seek out a banker who tries to think of creative ways to refinance loans so payments are smaller. Also, you need a banker who can involve other professionals from the bank to assist in developing strategies to improve your cash-flow situation.

- **Lawyer:** An inexperienced lawyer may suggest you begin as a sole proprietor because you are only one person and are just getting started. That's okay if you are writing business plans, but if you are a computer programmer or finance consultant and your advice leads to the company losing money, a client might

LLC: Think About It

A strategic partner of mine wrote a customized collection software program that billed a client's clients for a variety of products and services. The client was happy with the demo and the developer installed it. Unfortunately, my business associate wasn't told about another piece of software that needed to be integrated with it in order for bills to go out. One day the bank called my associate's client and said they were over-drawn and that they couldn't run payroll. The client blamed my associate and sued him, believing he was at fault. Unfortunately, my associate lost his case, but, because his attorney and accountant understood the type of risk my associate undertakes with each project, they had suggested that he incorporate as a limited liability corporation (LLC), which shielded his assets when he was successfully sued.

file a lawsuit and, because you are not incorporated, the client could take your personal assets if you lose. You want to make sure that your lawyer is smart enough to speak with your accountant and, possibly, a tax attorney to make the best recommendation about how to legally protect yourself.

4. Are their fees reasonable? You shouldn't be shy about asking for service provider's fees up front. Make sure the charges are comparable to what others charge in your region.

- **Accountant:** I don't believe any startup consultant needs one of the national accounting firms, but many consultants had used a national firm for their prior employers or knew someone at a large firm. When companies pick a national accounting firm, they are paying for the name in many cases. Unless you are looking to raise capital from venture capitalists or run a medium-size or large company, where having a big accounting firm is like getting the Good Housekeeping seal of approval, then you are spending money unnecessarily.

With the amount you will pay for a senior associate or manager (a step below partner) at a large accounting firm, you can engage a partner at a smaller firm. Very often, a partner at a small firm is a former manager at a big firm.

Ask the accountants if they are going to charge you every time they pick up the telephone or whether they will provide a set price for certain services. Many consultants are often shocked when they receive a bill that includes charges for each phone call to their accountant because most consultants charge by the project or work on retainer and don't charge for everything they do for a client.

- **Lawyer:** As with accountants, buying the services of a lawyer from a big regional or national firm is overkill unless you are trying to raise capital or planning to buy a larger consulting practice. Most corporate attorneys at small regional firms either came from large regional or national firms or from medium and large companies. Their fees, in most cases, are half that of a large firm.

    You must understand how your lawyer charges and let him or her know about your expectations. Read every bill and don't hesitate to ask questions. There are times you are charged for services that you didn't ask for because the lawyer thought it was necessary. Require sign-off on everything the lawyer is working on so that you maintain financial control.

I interviewed Steve Dubow, a partner at Blank, Rome, Cominsky and McCauley, who has an undergraduate degree from the University of Pennsylvania's Wharton School of Business and a law degree from Villanova

> *A colleague of mine needed boilerplate contracts to present to future clients. I suggested an independent legal practitioner to handle the assignment, but my colleague said he didn't want to use anyone second-rate or tell clients his contracts were developed by an unknown firm. Before I could tell my colleague that the attorney I was recommending was a semi-retired partner of a large firm, he cut me off. When he got a bill for $5,000 for a job that should have cost less than $1,000, he was in a state of shock.*

University. I asked him what a consultant should look for when hiring an attorney and what attorneys should be used for.

Question: What criteria should a consultant use when selecting an attorney?

Response: Obtain the level of experience with respect to the matter and obtain examples of work done in the area. Seek client references. Determine promptness in responding to clients. Determine compatibility with prospective clients.

Question: Should a consultant insist on having a partner handle his or her legal matters?

Response: It depends on the sophistication of the project. An associate may be able to handle the matter, but a partner should supervise the associate and be familiar with the matter.

Question: What type of legal work should consultants hire attorneys to do for them that they shouldn't do themselves?

Response: Hire an attorney to do documentation of acquisitions or investments, securities work, or review of contracts. The relationship between the attorney and the consultant should be collaborative.

Question: Should a consultant have an attorney develop a different contract for every engagement or one boilerplate contract that can be massaged for each project?

Response: There should be a template that is modified to fit the particular assignment but the basics will repeat in each assignment.

- **Banker:** Small banks are usually more suited to consultants and realize that too many fees will drive away business. Community banks welcome startup consulting firms and provide home equity and signature lines of credit.

5. Will they work with me financially if I can't afford their full fees in the beginning? If you do a good job of selling yourself, the company, and the industry, most professionals will work out suitable payment arrangements.

- **Accountant:** Accounting firms have flexibility because they charge for their time. These professionals always budget for a certain amount of low- or no-fee time for companies they believe have potential.
- **Lawyer:** Like accounting firms, lawyers can provide flexible payment terms. If the firm believes you are capable of building a solid practice and will use the law firm for corporate and business work, and would encourage other colleagues to use the firm, they will work with you.
- **Banker:** Bankers are always looking for new business and community banks like consulting businesses because they see very little risk and lots of opportunity for small loans backed up with quality assets. In order to attract new business customers, they provide a variety of low- to no-fee programs.

> *When I started my business, my bank gave me a $30,000 line of credit. If you are offered a line of credit when you start, take it. Use the line of credit instead of the cash in your bank account. You get the write-off, you establish credit, and you conserve your hard cash until you attract clients.*

The Advantages of Planning Well

A friend of mine started a software development company and was trying to raise capital. He went to a big accounting firm and made a presentation to a couple of the partners. They were so impressed with his experience, attention to detail, and plan for developing the company that they agreed to provide $10,000 worth of free services until he raised the money. They even offered to introduce him to some private investors. The firm also agreed not to charge him anything if any money was raised.

Inside or Outside?

A colleague of mine started a consulting firm specializing in transportation logistics because his employer, on the advice of a consultant, had decided to eliminate my colleague's group. Fortunately for my colleague, the employer was going to need help transitioning to an outsource group and my client demonstrated to his former employer that he would be the ideal outsourced "chief logistics officer." He ended up receiving a monthly retainer to work with vendors to manage logistics.

A friend of mine used a big law firm to close a deal with a group of angel investors. The lawyer involved had worked many years with the venture community and entrepreneurial companies. He liked the deal and agreed to wave his up-front fees, and also assigned a junior lawyer to handle the uncomplicated parts of the transaction. My friend received top-flight big name support for the cost of a lesser-known attorney and firm.

6. What do their clients say about them? Ask service providers for references and contact those references to make sure the service provider lives up to its billing. Ask other service providers to recommend professionals outside of their field. Ask an accountant to recommend a lawyer and vice versa. Professional service providers have experience working with each other and they don't want to make a bad recommendation.

7. When clients have left them, what were the reasons? Always try to find and speak with the clients who have left service providers that you are considering. There are many reasons clients leave and a lot of them don't have anything to do with performance. Personalities and the ways of doing business may not have matched.

8. Will they invite me to events even though I am a sole practitioner? Accounting firms, law firms, and banks look at consultants as good sources of potential deal flow. They believe that, if they do a good job for you, you will recommend them to your clients.

9. Will a seasoned executive be assigned to us or will we be used to allow junior executives to cut their teeth? Most firms of any size will assign a partner to handle complex issues and an associate to handle the smaller issues. Many

Helping Incrementally

One of my clients is Frank Masterangelo, president of The Bancorp, who was interviewed in this chapter. One of the things I notice that Frank does well is connecting his customers with other customers to do business. At the end of the day, practically every good service provider knows his or her craft. The question then becomes, what is the incremental value they bring to your company? Focusing on bringing incremental value beyond your area of expertise is as important for you as it is for the advisors you choose.

times the associates will have developed an area of expertise that the partner doesn't have and can be more valuable. It is important to know that an experienced executive has worked with your type of consultancy. If you want an idea of the level of service, look at the provider's business card to find out whether he or she lists a home telephone, pager, and car phone number on his or her card. If a pager and car phone number are listed, you know you will receive superior service.

- **Accountant:** Partners of accounting firms will assign junior people to audits, but will work with the client on personal and corporate tax strategies that determine the company's corporate structure.
- **Lawyer:** Look for attorneys who don't charge every time a question is asked and who know when and where to use an associate to save the client money.
- **Banker:** The larger the amount of the loan, the more senior the bank official handling the loan should be. If the company is borrowing a small amount, the banker that you are dealing with may be junior, but he probably answers to someone senior. Most community banks will assign someone senior because they don't have a lot of overhead.

Experienced bankers usually have a deep database of contacts. Use these contacts to help your company.

10. Will they introduce us to their other clients who can potentially bring us business? All good service professionals should have a diverse and large database of contacts. Such a contact source is an extra value that they can add. If all else between professionals under consideration is equal, choose the one who can open doors for new business, and provide advice and capital.

There are banks, accounting, and law firms that hold seminars for their clients on a wide range of topics and bring in other service providers who are expert in fields they know little about. These seminars usually attract potential new business.

> *A banker I had known for years went out of her way to network with a variety of companies. Clients joined her bank just for the introductions she made for them that opened up doors for new business.*

Finding Good Outside Professionals

If you don't have any business contacts that can give you recommendations, I would suggest you do the following:

- **Accountant:** Contact the local chamber of commerce/business organizations and ask your attorney and banker. Ask other business owners whom they use and what they like about them.
- **Lawyer:** Contact the local bar association and ask your accountant and banker.
- **Banker:** Because accountants deal with finances, they are a good source for recommending banks and bankers. Also, contact the regional office of the Small Business Administration and any entrepreneurial/business organizations in the region.

The one group that I haven't yet addressed in this chapter is financial planners/insurance agents. The same criteria you would use to judge accountants, bankers, and lawyers should be used for this group. You definitely need to find a good financial planner/insurance agent to help you decide types and sizes of coverage you need and how to plan for your financial future now that you don't have a company pension to fall back on, but I have found that I am not in continuous contact with my financial planner/insurance agent.

I interviewed Oscar L. Mestre, CLU, ChFC, who has been in the financial services industry since March 1982. He graduated from the University of Delaware with a BSBA in 1981, and received the Chartered Life Underwriter (CLU) and Chartered Financial Consultant (ChFC) professional designations from the American College in 1988.

Question: What types of insurance should a consultant buy when getting started?

Response: You should definitely buy disability income and life insurance to the degree you need it. Disability insurance is most difficult to get because you need a track record. Most times you need a track record of at least one year's earning in order for an insurance company to underwrite. If you know you are leaving a company, that is the time to apply so you are covered. Finally, you need health insurance, unless your spouse has it.

Question: How much money should a consultant budget for various insurance policies?

Response: It depends on how much you are trying to secure. You should budget a couple of thousand dollars just for disability and life, and for health insurance you are looking at $8,000 to $10,000 per year for a family or around $3,000 to $4,000 for an individual.

Question: When should a consultant set up a retirement plan?

Response: I think you should set it up as fast as humanly possible. Keep in mind the old saying, "If it is to be, it is up to me." Once you leave the comforts of an employer, you have to do it for yourself. The earlier you get into the habit of saving, the better off you will be.

Question: What type of retirement plan should the consultant set up?

Response: The best plan is a Simplified Employee Pension (SEP). Once you get into a bigger consulting practice, then you can talk about a profit-sharing plan.

Question: What percentage of income should a consultant put away for retirement?

Response: The savings rule of thumb is to put away between 10 to 20 percent per year in order to meet your future income needs. You should first try to max out on the amount you can contribute to retirement plans on a before-tax basis. Thereafter, make up the difference on an after-tax basis.

Question: Where can a consultant purchase the most economical health-care plan?

Response: Usually through a chamber of commerce or trade association plan.

Question: What is disability insurance and why should you have it and how much should you buy?

Response: It is a coverage that protects against the loss of ability to work and earn money. The rule of thumb is 60 percent of one's gross income if possible. The monthly amount insured will depend on the specific insurance company used. Aside from age, smoking status, and gender, they take into consideration what you do and where you work.

Question: How much life insurance should one buy and what type of life insurance?

Response: On average you should have as much life insurance as you need to pay off your debts and enough to continue your income for five to ten years to support your family. That would be the bare minimum. In a startup, you should buy a term insurance policy, because it will be the most economical. As cash flow improves, you may want to consider a variable life insurance policy as it will not only provide proceeds in case of death, it will also provide a tax-advantaged means to accumulate funds to supplement future income needs.

Question: Do you need to buy separate insurance for your car if you are using it for business or do you need to notify your insurance company that you are using your vehicle primarily for business?

Response: You need to notify your insurance company if you are using your car for consulting because there are different rates.

Question: Should you buy personal liability insurance and, if so, how much should one buy?

Response: You should also buy errors and omissions insurance. If you are giving advice it is important to have because of our litigation-happy society.

Chapter Key Points

Don't just select friends, acquaintances, or pick someone out of the telephone book to provide you with banking, accounting, legal support, and financial planning/insurance. You want professionals who:

- understand your business;
- provide a high level of service;

- have a strong network of contacts to make introductions on your behalf.

Once you have narrowed down your choices, make
sure to ask them for references. Do a little bit of
background checking, and make sure their clients
are happy with them.

SETTING UP YOUR OFFICE

MAKING YOUR WORKPLACE PRODUCTIVE ◄

One of the most enjoyable experiences of starting your consulting business is setting up your office. Buying everything you'll need to run your business is exciting. I firmly believe that everyone should try to operate out of his or her home until the business outgrows your house or your significant other decides you are in the way.

Before you start shopping on-line or running to your nearest business supply super store, however, you need to make a list of everything you need. I am sure you are wondering why I am devoting an entire chapter about how to set up an office. It's because many people I know who started a business out of their home wasted a lot of time and energy because they didn't think through what they would need and were ill-prepared to support their clients.

Below is a checklist of 35 must-have items that you will need to start your business. If you don't want to waste time making several trips to an office supply store and want to take advantage of discounts offered by on-line stores, I suggest you go to www.staples.com, www.officedepot.com, and www.officemax.com.

Office Necessities

From the experience of many people, here are some of the things you'll need to get your business up and running.

Technology

- Desktop computer
- Laptop computer
- Digital organizer
- Business card scanner
- Printer/fax/copier
- Mobile phone
- Telephone
- Telephone headphones
- Computer headphones
- Electronic writing tablets
- Shredder
- Binding machine
- Electric pencil sharpener

Furniture

- Desk
- Chair
- Bookshelf
- Supply shelf
- Mobile file cabinets
- Trash can
- Fireproof safe

Office Supplies

- Pens
- Pencils
- Paper clips
- Writing tablets

- Stapler
- Staple puller
- Letter and large envelopes
- Printer ink or toner cartridges
- Scissors
- Rewritable CD-ROMs
- Floppy disks

Software

- Operating system
- Accounting software
- Antivirus software
- Remote-access software

Tips on What to Buy

I don't think you need advice on everything on the list, especially office supplies, but I will provide you with suggestions regarding technology and software based on my own experience and with advice from Randy Feldman, President of Future Business Solutions. Randy has 16 years of information-systems experience. He has developed, implemented, and maintained computer systems and Web sites for national and international companies including Aetna US Healthcare, ECRI, and Vanguard. Randy has a B.S. degree in Chemical Engineering and a Master's degree in computer science from Pennsylvania State University.

Computers

Although office supply stores sell computers, everyone has personal preferences about the type of computer they are most comfortable with. In order to get the computer system that will serve you and your business without investing in unnecessary "bells and whistles," I suggest visiting sites such as www.dell.com, www.ibm.com, www.hp.com, www.toshiba.com, www.gateway.com, and www.apple.com.

Your computer will be one of the most expensive investments you make, and the type of computer you buy depends on a few factors that must be taken into consideration:

- What type of work do you plan to use the computer for?
- Will you work at one office or travel with the computer to different locations to work?
- Do you have a budget for the equipment?
- What kind of support do you have or need to set up and maintain the computer?

The answers to these and a few other questions will help you determine what you should buy. If you plan to set up an office and don't plan on working abroad, then a workstation or desktop computer will be the best solution. If you need to travel and take your work with you, a laptop or notebook would be appropriate.

The difference between a laptop computer and a notebook generally refers to the size and weight, with some

Internet Telephony

My wife and I have a home in Panama City, Panama. We absolutely have to have a laptop computer in order to run our business. Because telephone rates calling to the United States are about a $1 a minute, we needed a laptop that would have the capability to use Internet telephony. We had to make sure that our computer could make and take telephone calls. Our laptop allows us to run our business no matter where we are, and the ability to use Internet telephony saves me about 95 percent of the cost of a call to the United States, or $500 in telephone bills each time we are away, which is twice a year. That savings means I am practically getting my laptop for free.

variations in features like a built-in CD-ROM or one you need to attach to a docking station of some sort.

Once you decide on whether you need a laptop or a desktop model, you have to determine what kind of work you plan to do. If you plan to do professional design and graphics work or operate large or complex databases, develop and test programs, or similar resource-intensive work, then you will want to get the fastest and highest capacity computer you can afford. If you plan to use it mainly for communication, documentation, and standard office applications, then a more cost-effective choice, and not necessarily the fastest and most equipped with enhanced features, is required. Look for choices that include software that may help you get productive right away, like Microsoft Office and other packages.

Is one make or model better than another? The computer manufacturers are all very competitive today. Many of the companies use common boards and components, and allow you to mix and match features. The choice of whether you build or buy, and where you purchase your computer, depends on several factors:

- Building a computer will save you money, and you can select brand-name and quality components from the Internet, computer shows, and retailers.
- The leading computer suppliers like Compaq, HP, Toshiba, Gateway, Dell, Micron, and others sell through retailers, vendors, and the Internet. You need to check them to find your best price/performance, and evaluate the ability to get service and support.
- Weigh the need for support and service heavily; this will help you decide if you should order direct or shop at Staples or OfficeMax so that you have a place to go to get support. If you have a qualified local

computer store or larger ones like CompUSA or Micro Center, you may want to check them out for product and price comparisons in person.

- Check consumer reports and personal computer magazines and journals to read about evaluations and testing done on computers. This will help you decide what brand you want to buy.
- Check the warranty and special offers on different models and packages.
- Make sure you compare the price of packages with all the equipment you need, including a monitor, printer, and other peripherals.

What should one expect to spend on a desktop computer?
The price range today for a personal computer ranges from what it costs to build your own, to the best system from a leading manufacturer. You can build an excellent computer with brand-name and compatible components for approximately $750.00. You can purchase brand-name computers and packages from $500.00 to about $2,000.00, depending on features, performance, and extras. Laptop and notebook computers range from about $750.00 to $3,500.00. Once you decide on your needs, you can shop for the best computer or package in the category you want.

What should one expect to spend on a laptop computer?
Laptops are generally more expensive than desktops for the same features and performance. However, they allow you to work in a variety of places with no sacrifice in capability. There are many brands and models of laptops, and the quantity and availability change rapidly. Shop around the Internet for information and promotions, and check retail stores as well. As I said, laptop and notebook computers range from about $750.00 to $3,500.00, but I have gone on auction sites, such as Ubid (www.ubid.com), and

saved as much as 25 percent off the retail price of a computer.

How much memory and hard-drive space should one buy? Today, memory is inexpensive and disk space costs a fraction of what it used to. Maximize both of these in your purchase. Generally, the disk space offered today is more than you will use during the life of the computer. You should get a minimum of ten gigabytes of hard-disk space unless you are purchasing a special package and are sure of your data needs.

Memory is more critical in the performance of your computer. With the aggressive operating systems today, you should get a minimum of 128 MB of RAM in your computer. Expand this at the time of purchase or as soon as your budget allows to the maximum your computer will hold. Consider the amount and expandability of memory when you make your computer purchase.

Should you purchase a warranty for your computers? Most computers come with a manufacturer's warranty and other protection. Depending on what you buy, try to cover all the components and your computer for up to three years. This will basically cover you for the useful life of the computer, and will not likely be a great additional expense. Try to stick with extensions of warranties from the vendor or manufacturer. The reliability of computer equipment is very high and continually improving. Look to the available consumer information for a good balance of warranty and costs, and let the system you need take priority and the warranty coverage come second.

Software

Every computer comes with some type of operating system (OS), whether it's Microsoft or Apple. The question is, what type of software will you need to operate your business?

Future Business Solutions Advice: The software you buy depends greatly on what you need to do with the computer. There are four types of software you should purchase.

1. Business Function Software. Always buy a complete suite of office products like Microsoft Office Professional, which includes a word processor, spreadsheet program, database tools, presentation software, and other utilities. You will want to buy development and programming tools, depending on the work you plan to do, as well as other special-purpose software.

2. Security Software. Include software to maintain your computer like Norton SystemWorks (from Symantec) or McAfee's Internet Security, and a means to back up your data. Some of this software may be included when you purchase a computer package. If you build your own, make sure you buy an operating system and all the different software you need to do your work, keep your computer in good condition, and back up your data and information.

Don't skimp on buying security software. Any time you install software from the Internet or from a disk or CD of questionable origin, you run the risk of a virus or creating a doorway for intrusion. You need to run virus protection software that monitors all the ways damaging software can be introduced into your system. If you have your computer in an office where you need to ensure against unauthorized use, you will also need to install and activate hardware and software password protection schemes.

Most of the leading packages take care of all this for you. When you connect to the Internet, you will need to protect your computer by installing a firewall, which blocks and hides direct access to your computer from Internet users. You can manage without a firewall for occasional use of the Internet and regular dial-up usage. However, once you begin to remain connected for longer periods of time and for more resources, you will need to install protection software and a personal firewall or more to help eliminate malicious attacks.

3. Accounting. Intuit's Quicken Accounting Software and Peach Tree Accounting are the top two choices. Both allow you to keep track of expenses, bill customers, and create reports. I personally recommend Quicken because, when you prepare to do your taxes, you can buy Intuit's TurboTax tax filing software, which will link with Quicken to pull out the pertinent information. This will save you time and improve your reporting accuracy.

4. Remote Access. I highly recommend that all my clients buy a product called PC Anywhere, which was developed by Symantec. This software allows users who are not in their offices to retrieve files remotely from their desktop computers at their offices. When I have forgotten a file I need for a meeting with a client, I've been able to access it where I was, without having to return to my office.

Printer

There are a variety of printers you can buy, but I strongly suggest purchasing a Hewlett Packard Laser Jet with fax, scanning, and paper printer capabilities. Although these products cost upwards of $500 compared to a standard printer, which can be found for under $100, you will find that you need all four technologies, and it is better to have them all in one machine. Plus laser cartridges are more economical than ink cartridges.

Buying a Printer

Future Business Solution Advice: There are five pieces of advice I give my clients when they're deciding which printer to buy:

- If you need to produce quality printouts for publication or distribution, you need to buy a laser printer.
- If you need general-purpose printing and drafts, you should buy an inkjet printer.
- If you do graphics and color work, you need to buy a color inkjet or color laser for professional finishing.
- If you are setting up an office and want to optimize your capabilities in a small space, consider the combination printer/copier/scanner/fax machines from HP or other vendors. These offer excellent quality and usability at a competitive price.
- Stick with a name-brand printer for which you can easily get supplies and service. You should not buy a printer that requires special paper for standard printing. Size and features vary from model to model, so do comparison shopping at your local office store, and research the models just as you would for a computer.

Connecting to the Outside World

Now that you have your office set up, you need to buy telecommunication services so you can communicate with clients and your personal computer anytime and anywhere. You will need to purchase the following services:

- Local telephone service
- Long-distance service
- Mobile telephone service
- Internet access

The following interview is with Dr. Scott Snyder, one of the United States's leading experts on telecommunications and Internet services.

Scott Snyder (President and CTO) has more than 14 years of experience in satellite and ground based communications with General Electric and Lockheed Martin. Recognized as one of the premier system architects in the company, he has extensive experience working on the leading edge of telecommunications systems and products including broadband networks, satellite networks, mobile systems, virtual private networks, and the Internet. Dr. Snyder has lectured at MIT, the University of Pennsylvania, and RIT on new product development, product optimization, and telecommunications. Dr. Snyder earned his B.S., M.S., and Ph.D. in Systems Engineering from The University of Pennsylvania and has an executive degree from the USC in Telecommunications Management.

Question: Should an independent consultant use his or her local carrier for local and long-distance telephone calls?

Response: Check in your area to find out who offers what. It depends on the state. Verizon, for example, can only get long distance in a couple of states, although they are trying to get approval in other states. Your options are limited for local service. It really depends on the market. AT&T in Denver, through their cable service, is offering local and long distance and they are very competitive with the local Bell. RCN in New Jersey is like AT&T and is very competitive with the local Bell carriers.

For long distance there're about four big companies: ATT, Quest, World Com, and Sprint. Then there are approximately 25 carriers such as Global Crossing and RSL. You can shop around. It is a fairly defined service. You might get worse customer service and billing services from the smaller companies.

Then there is IP over the Internet. You probably don't want to use it for important calls where quality of interaction is important. For run-of-the-mill calls, IP calls are good. I suggest using IP telephony providers like Net2Phone calling cards when traveling.

Question: If you decide to shop for your telephone supplier, what criteria should you use to determine who can give you the best service at the best price?

Response: One of the things we do at Omnichoice is look at pricing. We check the monthly charge, minimum charges, and other hidden charges. Don't just look at the per-minute charge. Look at the quality of the service. I'm not talking about the technology, but the customer service. We have accumulated information on how people rate other carriers. You can go to JD Powers to get this information as well.

It becomes more confusing when companies bundle these services. You then have to take apart these plans and figure out which is the best service for you.

Question: Does your geographic location play a part in the type of services you can get and how much you have to pay for them?

Response: Absolutely! Some areas are much more competitive than others. In New York there are lots of options. If you go to Peoria there may be one option. The competition follows the money.

Many local phone companies offer value-added services such as intercom services and call forwarding.

Question: What type of criteria should I use for determining the appropriate Internet carrier and hosting service?

Response: When you are looking at an Internet connection, you want to look at availability. You need to see if you can get high-speed access. If you aren't transferring a lot of data, that isn't a problem. If you do send lots of data, such as PowerPoint presentations and lots of material, then you might want to look at satellite, cable, ISDN, and DSL. You need to check availability.

For example, if you are farther than 15,000 feet from a switch, then DSL is hard to get and, even if you can get DSL, it might not be worth it because the degradation is so bad. Satellite is only in its infancy and there are only a couple of players in that market. It's good, however, if you can't get DSL or cable. Satellite costs about $70 per month.

Security is a big issue with cable. If all of your neighbors are on cable modem then you are all sharing the same cable and I would recommend a firewall. It would be very easy for neighbors to hack into your computer if they got your IP address.

Depending on what type of business you are in, four types of hosting are available: virtual, dedicated, co-location, and managed. Virtual is best for a consultant. You are actually sharing an IP address and a server with other companies, although your customer doesn't know that. It may slow down your site. Using a virtual server costs only around $20 a month.

Question: Are all the hosting services the same in terms of technology capability?

Response: With hosting, you want to look at the equipment they are using. There are three tiers. With Tier One

Go Local

Don't go with a large Web-hosting company. Go with a company that is in your region that will allow you to call and speak to the president. The larger the company, the longer the wait for customer service, which anyone who has used Earthlink or Verio knows. One of the sites I owned that was hosted by a large provider went down and it was hours before I could speak to someone to check on the server and reboot it. On my other sites I use a small provider and, when a site goes down, within minutes I can speak to someone and they will, literally, go over to the server and reboot it. If the Internet is a major part of your business, go with someone small.

(companies like MCI), your performance is going to be much better than the other two tiers. A Tier Two has to connect to a Tier One, so Tier Two and Tier Three don't provide as good a service because the connection isn't as quick and efficient. You also want to know if the company provides 24/7 service. You may not want your site to go down on a Sunday and find that no one is available to fix your problem until Monday and lose business opportunities.

Question: Does one's own technology capability on both telephone and Internet factor into which providers are the best matches?

Response: No! The standards have become so prevalent that it shouldn't be a problem. Usually you need a certain type of equipment to take advantage of certain services.

Chapter Key Points

A consultant's time is money. Don't waste a lot of time buying supplies, furniture, and equipment piecemeal. Remember to do the following:
- Take the list we provide in this book and put it into a spreadsheet.
- Buy quality so you won't have to replace it within three to four years.
- Don't waste time going to stores when you can buy on-line.

Also, shop around for your telecommunications services. Buy two Internet connections and make sure one of them has international dial up because at some point you will need it. Finally, get yourself a quality chair because you will be spending a lot of time sitting in it.

LET PROSPECTS KNOW YOU EXIST

A *former client of mine left her company after it was bought by a rival and decided to take the outplacement package that they offered her. According to her peers in her old company, Beth was a world-class expert on developing innovative products for the auto insurance industry. Beth had developed and documented a 25-step process for creating new products that could be used in any industry.*

Three months after Beth left her company, she called me. When I asked her how her new venture was going, she said she hadn't made one sales call, let alone gotten a new client. Beth was one of my biggest and best clients, so I asked her to e-mail me her marketing plan and offered to meet her for lunch. As smart and as knowledgeable as Beth was about developing new products, she had no experience and little understanding of how her great ideas became successfully sold products. She knew her marketing department developed an awareness campaign and that her company's sales force followed up with prospective clients, but she never took the time to understand how to get the attention of prospects in order to get face time to educate and sell them on her product.

Marketing You

You may be the world's most knowledgeable professional in your field, but if no one knows you, then to potential customers you do not exist. In Chapter 1, you read about the need for an overall business plan, which will give you a clear understanding of what you need to do to succeed. Developing a marketing plan is the next step to enhancing your chances of success. A marketing plan should have the following elements:

- Offering Description
- Industry
- Users
- Buyers
- Influencers
- Trade Organizations
- Geographic Target
- Marketing Tools
- Launch Plan
- Marketing Budget

I believe in short marketing plans because they are easy to follow and execute. The easier it is to execute your marketing plan, the better your chance of creating awareness about your service.

Marketing Plan Elements

I will describe each element of a marketing plan and, at the end of this chapter, provide a sample plan.

Offering Description. The offering description should be no more than three sentences, preferably one. It should roll off your tongue when you are in an elevator. A good test of whether your description of your company is easy to remember is to ask a child or your parents to describe what

Understanding Value

One of my clients was approached by an information technology company about teaming up to go after business. My client offered consulting in the distance learning area, and the information technology company offered a product that enabled companies to categorize all of their products so salespeople could match the best product with the need. It took us two visits and four hours to understand the value of this service because it wasn't clearly communicated. Within a year, the information technology company went out of business because no one could understand the value of their product.

you do. If they stumble looking for words, you can bet your prospects will, too.

Industry. If you go to the U.S. Census Bureau site (www.census.gov) and click on the section that provides information on various industries, you will see that there are over a thousand industries, not including the subcategories. You need to focus on a specific industry whether or not you believe your service can be used by any industry. Companies pay people for their expertise in what they do and the industry they do it for. Selecting a specific industry and, possibly, a sub-group of that industry makes it easier to develop an expertise, identify prospects, and keep your marketing costs to acceptable levels.

Users. Who needs your service? You need to figure out who has a pain for which you can supply the cure. For example, let's say you train telemarketing people on how to overcome objections and increase their sales performance. The telemarketing field has enormous turnover, ranging from 50 to 75 percent per year. Part of the reason is low pay, but the bigger reason is because people get tired of being rejected. You know there is a need, but in this case you know that low-paid people aren't going to hire you on

TheArtBiz

An example of a successful offering description: I am the CEO of a company called TheArtBiz and here is what we do: "We market and educate college and professional artists." That simple sentence tells what we do and whom we do it for. How long did it take to create that simple sentence? It took approximately eight weeks. It took so long because all of us tend to mention everything we do when describing ourselves. The more we mention, the less chance someone has of remembering what we do.

an individual basis to train them. Therefore, you have to know who in an organization would buy your services.

Buyers. No one is more important than the person who writes the checks. One mistake that many new consultants make is not focusing their time and attention on the people who decide how and with whom they spend money. A business associate of mine spent a lot of time getting to know the marketing director of a small company. In all the time he spent romancing this contact, he neglected to ask his contact what size budget he had and whether he had discretionary power to spend it with whomever he wanted. Unfortunately for my associate, all of the decisions were made by the marketing director's boss, the Vice President of Marketing, who considered the Director of Marketing a good implementer and never discussed or asked for input in vendor selection.

Influencers. This group is made up of inside and outside advisors to the buyers. Part of my consulting practice focuses on developing business plans for startup companies. The professionals I need to know are corporate attorneys and accountants because they are the first professionals a new entrepreneur usually retains and they are the ones the entrepreneur goes to for recommendations.

Trade Organizations. Defining your industry and the title of your target will clarify which trade associations to join to meet the right people. For example, if you provide a service that reduces electric costs for health-care organizations, you would target regional and national hospital associations and join the financial professionals' and facility managers' subgroups so you could meet the chief financial officers, treasurers, controllers, and maintenance managers.

Geographic Target. I haven't met the consultant yet who could market to the entire world, country, state, or half a state. Therefore, you have to choose a specific geographic region to start with and build from there. Don't spread yourself too thin. Get to know the target companies and influencers in your own region.

Marketing Tools. You can use a variety of marketing tools to promote your consultancy, but when you are just starting out you don't have a lot of money, so you need to be creative. I have found the following tools to be inexpensive and very cost- effective:

Books
How It Works: You develop a proposal, which is similar to a business plan, about writing a book on your area of expertise. Because you are a first-time author, the chances of obtaining an agent to represent you are remote. Buy a book called *Instruction Book for Writers: A Step-by-Step Guide to Publishing, Marketing, and Promoting Your Book* (Cornerstone Publishing) and write to all of the editors of the various business trade publishers such as Adams Media, Entrepreneur, John Wiley & Sons, McGraw-Hill, and Prentice Hall, to name a few.
Costs: The only cost is your time to develop the book. You don't write books to make money; you write books to

> *Writing a book is one of the best ways to differentiate yourself in the market. The vast majority of my clients hire me because the books I have written give me the aura of being an expert.*

enhance your stature in your industry and to differentiate your consultancy from competitors. A typical advance usually ranges from $1,500 to $10,000; you receive half up front and half when the manuscript is accepted.

Best Use: I have written four books because I have found that they have opened doors to new clients, strategic partners, and provided enhanced visibility with the local and national press.

Conferences

How It Works: Conferences are always looking for experts who are willing to speak for no fee. Contact the executive directors of the trade associations, chambers of commerce, and other business organizations you belong to.

Costs: The only costs are travel. Some conferences will pay your travel costs in lieu of paying an honorarium.

Best Use: Speaking to business leaders is a great way to establish your credibility and make new friends. Any time you are going to speak, send out a press release to notify local publishers.

Giveaways

How It Works: You can pick practically any item and give it away to clients. These can range from baseball caps and T-shirts (my personal favorites, because people wear them and become personal billboards for your service), to golf balls, pens, notebooks, and so on.

Costs: The cost depends on the size of the order, which can be as low as ten. The costs you incur are for the artwork, setup charges, and manufacturing.

Best Use: These are great gifts to give away at conferences and on your company's anniversary date. Notice I didn't say Christmas. People get so many gifts at Christmas that your gift can get lost in the deluge. Send giveaways at a time when people usually don't receive anything.

Direct Mail

How It Works: There are list service companies such as American List Council (www.amlist.com) that will assist in either renting or selling you a list.

Costs: The cost to rent or buy a list is based on the quality of the list, the difficulty in getting the list, the number of names to be bought, and the information you want to obtain, such as name, position, company, address, telephone, fax, and, possibly, e-mail. E-mail addresses are still difficult to obtain. When buying a list, you have to pay a setup charge that usually runs approximately $300 and then $.10 to $1.00 a name.

Best Use: The best way to use a direct-mail list is to write a one-page letter to 500 prospects letting them know about your service and offering them something of value, such as free consultation or a book related to your area of expertise. You want to offer something of value so prospects will pick up the telephone and call you.

I interviewed Steve Emory, who has worked as a marketing strategist on both the client and agency sides of the direct-marketing business. For 29 years, he has produced winning direct response TV, direct mail, catalog, telemarketing, and most recently, Internet marketing and Site development, and e-mail campaigns for national advertiser clients. He began his career as a product manager at the Franklin Mint, and is the founder and CEO of Network-Direct and its new division, Eagle Email. He has extensive experience in the retail, insurance, and financial service industries.

Question: What is better for a consultant to use? Direct mail or opt-in e-mail?

Response: I would say direct mail is best for producing sales leads from "suspects," if used properly and if it is followed up by introductory telephone calls. "Suspects" are those people that you want to do business with, but that don't know it yet. Permission e-mail is best for dialoging with customers or prospects that know you. Direct mail isn't as intrusive, and is an accepted mainstream method of B2B communication. e-mail is still new and good targeted lists that you can rent are scarce. Plus, if you don't get clear-cut permission from busy executive decision makers (not an opt-in from a chance Web site visit), e-mail is considered to be very offensive and intrusive.

Question: What size campaign should a new consultant start with?

Response: It's a function of capacity and time management. If you work 40 hours a week and you are working for clients half the time, you need to budget how much time you have left to follow up on sales leads. If you are just starting with direct-mail sales prospecting, you shouldn't mail any more than 1,000 pieces. I would mail in small segments over two to four weeks, so you have time to follow up by telephone with people who respond and, more importantly, to follow up with the more than 99 percent that don't respond. Mailing in small segments also gives you time to see what type of feedback (if any) you get.

Assuming your mailer is produced in-house using Microsoft Word and your own stationery, if you get negative or no feedback, you can adjust the letter or other inserts in the mailer or simply stop mailing. Then you can reevaluate your goals, target audience, and the quality of the list you used, your offer (incentive to respond), and even your timing. Your timing could be good or bad based on the season, or your competition. If your initial mailing segment is successful, you will need the extra time to give your undivided attention to respondents before you resume mailing the balance of your list.

Question: Should consultants call a mail-list house such as Dun & Bradstreet or Info USA and just buy targeted lists and handle the mailing themselves?

Response: Both companies and others are very reputable and offer lots of list experience. This is critical in helping you rent intelligently, based on the successes and failures of those businesses that preceded you (renting lists) with similar products and services. If you just mail a rented list one time, you will probably get very little response. You need to mix in your personal contacts, and you need to sustain contact over a period of time to establish credibility with your company and product. Also, don't forget that you are competing for attention in your target audience's already crowded mailbox.

Question: What kind of returns can a consultant expect on a direct-mail campaign?

Response: Don't expect better than 1 percent because there is too much mailbox clutter. Most people have a negative reaction to receiving mail from people they don't know. If you want to put your best foot forward with your introductory mailing, send it first class. If I receive something that is sent bulk mail, it goes directly in the "round" file with no second thought. I at least will quickly skim first-class mail.

Question: What kind of results can a consultant expect on an e-mail campaign?

Response: There are many misconceptions about "what the response will be to an e-mail campaign." I have conducted head-to-head tests (between mail and e-mail) when the goal was to drive retail store traffic, and the mail received more responses. However, it depends a great deal on the

> *E*-mail messages should never be more than one screen in length. The E-mail message should be brief but enticing enough to get readers to open an attachment or go to a Web site for more information. The exception to this is an e-mail newsletter, which might scroll for several pages, but few people have the patience to scroll and read the entire piece.

list and the level of permission granted. When the goal is to drive traffic to a Web site, e-mailers typically expect to receive a five to 10 times greater response than direct mail delivers.

Question: How long is an effective letter or an e-mail message?

Response: For a one-step direct-mail sales package, the answer is "as long as it takes" because you are asking for the order in the package. In a two-step lead-generation package, a one-page letter is the norm. It's OK for copy to run over to the back of a single sheet of paper if it's a compelling letter.

Question: What should a consultant budget for a direct-mail campaign?

Response: For a professional outsourced package, you should budget $500 to $750 per thousand pieces if you mail to over 50,000 people. If you are mailing to fewer, you can double that price. That figure includes buying the list, printing, personalization, mailing, and postage. In addition, if you do more than write your own sales letter, creating the design, photography, and copyrighting of a direct-mail package by professionals can cost anywhere from $5,000 to $20,000 or more, depending on whether you use a freelancer or an ad agency.

Question: What should a consultant budget for an e-mail campaign?

Response: For e-mail you are going to pay $200 to $300 per thousand names rented for the list. You will probably pay $25 to $50 per thousand to push it out and $3,000 to $4,000 to set up the list on a mail server. You can create your own message and save money if you send the e-mail out in plain-text format. Plan to spend $500 to $3,500 to create an effective HTML e-mail, and lots more for any form of rich media e-mail (i.e., audio or video). The more innovative the format, in combination with the right list, subject line, content, and offer, the better the response.

Question: What questions should one ask when buying a mailing or e-mailing list?

Response: How is the list maintained? How do you integrate changes of addresses and e-mail addresses? How recently were people added to the list? Who else is using this list and how frequently are they using the list? Also ask how the list has performed for other users.

If you are conducting a targeted mailing you also need title, job function, and the telephone number, along with the address. You need to be able to follow up with telephone calls. Never rent a list without individual names, and with B2B prospecting, I also wouldn't rent a list without valid and up-to-date telephone numbers. If you're on a tight budget, you can compile your own list of companies from business directories and a telephone book for free.

Remember that people on lists "turn over" (business change of address) as much as 50 percent each year. That is why you need to know how often the list is updated.

Question: What criteria should a buyer of direct-marketing services use to evaluate a direct-marketing firm or professional?

Response: Years of experience and related experience with other clients are a good starting point. If you are in the financial services industry, you want someone who understands the nuances of selling to decision makers in that industry. Even with this knowledge, there is no guarantee of success, so take every opportunity to stack the deck in your favor.

Question: For direct-mail or e-mail campaigns to be successful, how often do you have to run one?

Response: Continuity is the norm for success. Rarely can you mail just once. You need to educate your market about you and your service, and establish credibility. On a time continuum, responses typically will go down from one mailing to the next, using the same message, and selling the same service to the same list. Establish your maximum cost to acquire a new customer, and budget for the number of mailings you can afford, assuming very conservative response rates. E-mail is different, and people take it very personally.

We all expect lots of direct-mail pieces, but we don't expect, or want to receive, lots of unsolicited e-mails. You have to be careful with how often you send e-mail messages. Even if you use a permission-based source, be sure what you send has value and that they expect it.

Question: What is a reasonable percentage of bad addresses a buyer should expect?

Response: With e-mail, a 10 to 20 percent bounce rate on a monthly basis is not unusual. Bounces are a result of non-valid (expired and changed) e-mail addresses and full mailboxes. Another problem with e-mail is that people have multiple addresses and they may not look at one or more mailboxes as often as they do others. Few let you know they have cancelled an e-mail address and what their new address is.

With rented direct-mail lists, "clean" and current lists that are USPS "automatable" have a delivery rate in the high 90 percent range. Consumer lists that are a year or more old will have a 20 percent nondeliverable rate because of the high number of changes of address. Nondelivery of business lists more than one year old can be as high as 50 percent. To keep nondelivered mail to a minimum, direct mailers need to run their mail lists through the USPS National Change of Address cleaning software on a regular basis. This service is provided for a fee by an elite group of licensed suppliers throughout the United States. You can find those suppliers nearest you by contacting the USPS or the Direct Marketing Association (DMA) in New York.

Question: Can a buyer ask the seller of the list for a refund on the bad addresses and, if so, how much can one get back?

Response: You need to know what you are buying or renting up front. I have never received a refund for a list I'd bought, although I believe it has happened. You can avoid this issue by not renting from an unknown source that isn't established in the business. Contact your local or the national Direct Marketing Association and they can refer you to credible list-rental companies. Two of the best sources for renting business lists are Dun & Bradstreet and American Business International.

Question: What are the biggest mistakes people make when using direct mail to attract customers?

Response: They don't understand the economics of direct mail. They believe they have a good product and have rented the right list, but they underestimate the cost to acquire a new customer. What you spend depends on the selling price and profit margin for your product or service and how much you need to sell to achieve your return-on-investment goals.

E-mail is so popular because you can build your own permission list, send out messages quickly, at a fraction of the cost of direct mail, and receive results in about 48 hours. Consultants and all direct marketers should use an integrated approach to new business prospecting, using both direct and e-mail.

> *One of my information-technology clients insisted that he wanted to send out a direct-marketing piece to promote his business. I asked him how much money he had budgeted. When he told me, I said, "Unless you can run the campaign once a month for at least three months, you will be wasting your money." He didn't believe me, and, out of a mailing of 1,000, only 10 calls came in and seven were from vendors selling their own services. Consistency of message is key. If you can't afford it, don't do it.*

Question: What is the one piece of advice you would give someone who has never used direct mail or e-mail to advertise before?

Response: With direct mail, you have to know your average order value, your desired gross profit margin, and your allowable acquisition cost per order. This way you will know what you can afford to spend to acquire each new customer. By building financial models using various pro forma response and lead-to-sale conversion rates, you can "see" what type of mailing performance you need to be successful. When building pro formas, consider the "lifetime value" of each new customer, not just the dollar value of the original sale. A detailed mailing plan and budget that can be reviewed with your accountant in advance is a good idea.

With e-mail, the same tenets of direct mail hold true, but I would say the most important thing is to know your list. You need to know the level of permission granted. There is opt in and double opt in. Opt-in addresses are those compiled from Web site visits. As with direct mail, "compiled" lists are the poorest-performing lists. Many people who opt in don't realize they opt in for solicitations from sources other than the Web site they originally registered on. Double opt-in addresses are those that have also been e-mailed and forewarned that your intention is to send promotional e-mail in the future. Those receiving the double opt-in e-mail get a second chance to opt out before they are solicited. If you use a double opt-in process, you can expect as much as 50 percent to opt out, but those remaining are usually seriously interested.

Event Sponsorship
How It Works: All nonprofit organizations look for individuals and companies to sponsor events. The events can range from seminars to sports teams to business and civic award

dinners. In order to sponsor an event you need to speak with the president or executive director of an organization. *Costs:* There is no set fee. Costs are determined by the number of people expected to attend an event, the prestige of the organization, and the cost to run the event and turn a profit for the organization. Sponsorship can range from $250 to thousands of dollars. Many organizations allow for multiple sponsorships to lessen the cost and allow more organizations to participate.

Best Use: A great way to build name recognition and to be considered a player in the business community. Try to sponsor events with organizations that reach your specific target market. The biggest mistake people make when sponsoring events is that they take a shotgun approach and try to hit a cross-section of business people, or they look for the least expensive events to sponsor, which tend to draw small numbers of the wrong people.

Fliers

How It Works: Develop a one-page advertisement that tells who you are, what you have to offer, and how to reach you. *Costs:* Fliers are one of the least expensive marketing tools. You need only your computer and paper.

Best Use: If you are selling a low-cost service that anyone can use, and image isn't as important as finding someone who can do a particular job, then a flier is a useful tool. Individuals who supply home-improvement consulting make good use of fliers. Many homeowners look for someone to oversee small construction projects or major renovations to a house, which has spawned a very lucrative building contracting consulting business for independent engineers and architects.

Newspaper Column

How It Works: Many newspapers and trade journals look for

subject-matter experts who are either willing to impart their knowledge for free (that is what 90 percent of publications look for) or willing to take a small fee, such as $25 to $50, per column. Most columns are no more than 500 words, and the most any newspaper would want would be a column a week. Rarely do newspapers want a weekly column. Most want a column only once every four to six weeks.

Costs: No cost.

Best Use: A great free way to build visibility and credibility. Over the last four years, I have received an average of a call a month from my columns for the Norristown, Pennsylvania, *Times-Herald* (www.timesherald.com), part of the Journal Register national chain of newspapers.

Organization Sponsorship

How It Works: This is similar to event sponsorship, except you are sponsoring an entire organization. Two of my business associates, Robin Neifield and Denise Zimmerman, started a marketing practice called NetPlus Marketing (www.netplusmarketing.com), which assists companies in marketing their products and services to the Internet. In order to create buzz and meet top-level marketing executives, they created and cosponsored an organization called the Internet Business Alliance, which died four years after they started it. Through the founding of that organization, however, they made contacts at a major Philadelphia law firm and a major national newspaper, which both ended up hiring them to develop their Internet strategies.

Costs: The cost to sponsor or cosponsor an organization can range from nothing more than putting in personal time, which for consultants is real money (because time is what you sell), to a combination of cash and time. The cash usually ranges from a low of $500 to as much as $10,000.

Best Use: It's a great way to meet people and develop relationships without having to overtly sell yourself. Find out about new organizations that are looking for sponsors or older organizations that are trying to reinvent themselves and need financial support.

Partner Endorsement

How It Works: There are companies that may be able to cross-sell your service as a way to show their clients and prospects that they can offer additional value and contacts. One of my clients is called BCS Solutions (www.bcssinc.com), which provides computer and software project-management consulting. I approached a regional accounting firm about partnering with my client and offering clients and prospective clients an operations audit that would include financial, management, and information systems. By partnering with my client, the accounting firm was able to play at the same level as national accounting firms.

Costs: In most cases, there is no cost. Some partners will ask for a 10 percent finder's fee if their profession allows them to accept it.

Best Use: Find partners where there will be mutual benefit. Many companies will tell you not to worry because you can't bring them new business because you offer something of value that they can leverage with their clients. That won't last for long, because the company will either develop the expertise themselves or find a partner that can bring them new business.

Print Advertisements

How It Works: Advertising in the print media is one of the oldest and most expensive ways of building visibility. You buy advertising space in a publication and hope that someone gives you a call or recognizes your name when you call them.

Costs: The costs can range from $100 for a one-time eighth-of-a-page advertisement in a local publication to tens of thousands of dollars for a national publication.

Best Use: If you can't afford to run an advertisement a minimum of 12 weeks, don't bother wasting your money. If you decide to do it, see what percentage of the readers would have an interest in your product. Most respected publications have hired outside firms to survey their readers to find out their interests and provide that information in their advertising packages.

Print Newsletters

How It Works: The writing and, in many cases, the need for graphics are the same as an on-line newsletter.

Costs: The costs for developing a print newsletter include typesetting and the actual printing. There is software available by Broderbund (www.broderbund.com) called My Brochure, which allows you to create and print out a newsletter on your own computer. The problem is that few personal computer printers can print heavier stock than computer paper, which means your newsletter will appear cheap. The cost for printing a minimum of 500 newsletters on 60- to 80-pound paper is typically around $500 to $1,000. If you have to hire a writer or purchase a service that provides completed copy, that can cost you another $200 to $500 per issue.

Best Use: My advice is to develop a quarterly on-line newsletter and see what clients have to say. If the response is good, send a paper version of the same newsletter out the month after the electronic version. This will allow you to stay in front of clients and prospects and also allow them to collect and pass around your information to others in their offices.

Public Relations

How It Works: The media is always looking for new stories because every day they need to fill their print pages, air time, and Web sites with new, interesting stories and information. The best way to get exposure if you are going to handle your own publications is to write a short, two- to three-paragraph e-mail to editors and writers offering to be an expert in a story or when you achieve something significant, such as winning an award or obtaining a major contract.

If you prefer not to handle your own public relations, hire an individual public relations consultant. Before you write the first check to a publicist, however, put on paper what you would like to accomplish and what you are willing to spend to accomplish it. Remember, publicists have no control over the media, even though many have good media contacts that trust their judgment about the value of the story they are proposing. The reason you hire a publicist is because that individual will know how to package you.

I paid a publicist $10,000 to market my second book, *Small Business Turnaround*, published by Adams Media. In one day, the publicist had me on two radio shows, Bloomberg Business Network, a business cable television show, and Cable News Network Financial News. They even got me on the back page of *Entrepreneur*, published by my current publisher, which helped me land the contract to write this book.

When hiring a publicist make sure the person has connections with the media you are interested in attracting. The publicist I hired for my book specialized in promoting books.

Costs: On average, a publicist can cost between $1,000 and $10,000 a month. I have hired publicists at lower fees and paid them incentives that potentially would make them 25 to 100 percent more than they quoted. In my marketing practice, I have provided public relations support and have offered my clients the opportunity to pay me a low up-

A client of mine hired a public relations firm to market her technology company. The person in charge of her account was a seasoned professional, but he didn't have any contacts in her field. Yes, she got media coverage, but she didn't get calls or noticed by the audience she was after.

front fee and incentives and it has worked well for me. Remember, PR is very difficult so don't expect anyone do it without an up-front fee.

Best Use: Don't waste writers' or editors' time with stories that you wouldn't want to read. If you or your publicist provides something of value, such as your expertise for a story or an introduction to an expert for a story, the media will call you back.

I interviewed Peter Key, who covers technology, venture capital, and nonprofits for the *Philadelphia Business Journal*. He has also worked at the *Indianapolis Star* and the *Press of Atlantic City*, and once wrote gags for *Hazel*, a syndicated cartoon panel created and drawn by his father, Ted Key. He has a B.A. in English and an M.B.A. from Penn State and lives in Philadelphia.

Question: How does a business get the attention of the media?

Response: You can send press releases, faxes, or e-mails or call the reporter (although I'd only recommend doing only one). Or you can do something that the media notices or hears about by word of mouth.

Question: Should a business hire a public relations firm to get the best results?

Response: Usually, yes! Because the businessperson is usually too busy building the business. You don't have to hire a big firm. You can get a consultant on retainer to do a good job.

Question: If yes, what are the characteristics you find in successful public relations people?

Response: They are honest. They don't promise anything they can't deliver. They are good relationship builders because they are honest. The reporter knows that he or she isn't getting junk from the person. The reporter knows the PR person can deliver. Any person who hires a PR person has to realize it's a marathon and not a sprint. It takes time to get results. Be happy with small results at first—a mention here, a notice there.

Question: If you can't afford a public relations person, what is the best way to attract media attention?

Response: First try to figure out what media would cover you. Figure out what they are interested in. e-mail the media about your availability to help with a story. Send information about people you hire or any new contracts you obtain.

Question: Should you write to an editor or to individual reporters?

Response: Initially, if you don't know which reporters to contact, you should go through the editor. If you know which reporters cover your area, then go directly to the reporter.

Question: What annoys a reporter the most that assures a business of not getting any attention?

Response: Constantly calling after sending e-mail, fax, and letter. Acting as though everything you send is important. Not being available, after promising to be available, to answer questions on a story.

Question: Should a businessperson target specific reporters and try to get to know them?

Response: Yes! This can take time. You have to provide the reporter a reason to get to know you, because so many people want to get to know the reporter.

Question: Does buying advertising in a newspaper increase your chances of getting newspaper coverage?

Vinegar and Sugar

I once worked for a very successful entrepreneur who felt that the amount of money he spent in advertising should have bought him free editorial coverage. My boss called the editor of the paper and threatened to pull his substantial advertising if the paper didn't write a story on his business. The editor told him to pound sand and my boss pulled the advertising. After weeks of declining sales, he gave up and began to advertise again. I called a writer at the paper and invited him to lunch with my boss and, after meeting my boss, he decided to do a story.

Response: No! Because the editorial departments are run separately from the advertising departments. When advertisers demand that a reporter write a story, it angers the reporter.

Seminars

How It Works: You develop a presentation for potential clients that comes across as educational. You make a mailing to prospects and offer them a gift to attend. Not something cheesy like a pen or a coffee mug, but a book related to your subject. If you are uncomfortable making presentations, invite prospects and clients to participate in a panel discussion that you could host.

Costs: The cost of running a seminar includes the following:

- **Invitations:** Invitations typically cost $500 for 1,000 invitations.
- **Postage:** Postage runs $.37 to $.60 an invitation, depending on the size of the invitation and the response card.
- **Presentation facility:** Pick a nice place, such as a quality hotel or conference center. This will cost between $500 and $1,000.
- **Handouts:** A handout is composed of the material discussed at the seminar. You should budget approx-

imately $1 a handout.

- **Meals:** Depending on whether you are having a breakfast, lunch, or dinner seminar, the cost will range from $5 a person to $35 a person on average. I always encourage clients to go with breakfast seminars, because people don't like their day disrupted by lunch seminars and usually have family or personal activities to attend in the evening.
- **Gifts:** The right gift, especially a well-written book on your area of consulting, will make a statement about your level of understanding and thinking related to your industry.

Best Use: The best way to attract prospects is to offer them a chance to speak at a seminar. There is nothing people like more than sharing their expertise. If you get three leading regional or national people to speak at a seminar you sponsor, it will reflect positively on you and people will want to do business with you because they believe you have clout.

I interviewed Nancy Michaels, co-author of *Off-the-Wall Marketing Ideas,* published by Adams Media in 2000, about the best ways to market a consulting practice. Nancy provides creative marketing consulting services and seminars to independent business owners and entrepreneurs. In a three-year span, Nancy conducted more than 600 in-store, hour-long consumer seminars, "How to Be a Big Fish in Any Pond: Memorable Marketing on a Shoestring," on behalf of Staples the Office Superstores, Inc. Nancy is the first recipient to win the Tom Peters WOW! Project Personified Award for her work at Staples. She has a B.S. in Television Production from Emerson College and an M.A. from Emerson in Behavioral and Organizational Behavior.

Question: What marketing tools provide the best results in the shortest period of time for new consultants?

Response: Publicity is the best way to get instant credibility, but it takes a lot of time to develop press relationships. You need a good angle that will grab the media's attention and you need to highly define it. I would urge consultants who are serious about their business to hire consultants to market them. You also need to develop a good relationship with a graphic arts firm to create a memorable image.

You want something that professionally represents you. Most small business owners want to save money in the beginning and I see that as a big mistake. I also discourage brochures, which I consider a huge waste of money.

Question: What is civic marketing and how can you use it to your advantage?

Response: There is nothing wrong with getting something out of any contribution you make to a nonprofit, whether it is time or money. This gesture can bring personal satisfaction as well as marketing opportunities because it can open doors with potential clients. I like doing business with companies who are making a contribution. It is the responsibility of the business owner to let customers know what you are committed to. You need to pick a cause you have a personal connection with because you have a vested interest and are passionate about it.

Question: How much should someone budget to market his or her service?

Response: You should make a projection of what you think you will bring in and plan to spend 10 to 15 percent of that figure. You probably should spend even more in the beginning, because you need to target groups that fit the profile of the clients you are after.

Question: Should you hire a professional or do it yourself?

Response: If you can afford to hire someone, you can give yourself a jump-start. I wouldn't totally turn it over to someone. If you enjoy it, then you should do it, but I would suggest getting someone to handle public relations and media.

Question: What are the pros and cons of hiring a professional?

Response: Having someone else represent you who has relationships with the press suggests a more objective voice. The downside is, if you don't know how it works, then you might not know what you are getting. You should also get references. If you see someone mentioned in the media a lot who isn't a competitor, you might ask the person who he or she uses.

Question: What kind of experience should you look for in professionals to market a consulting practice?

Response: They should have a minimum of two years of real-world experience. That gives them time to have built relationships. You want someone who can pick up the phone and get someone to listen. When you speak with the media, you want to treat them like a business prospect. You also need to find out the best ways and times to communicate with them.

If you are hiring a marketing person, you need someone who sees the big picture. You want someone who responds to you quickly. I would be clear on what you want to achieve and how much you are willing to spend. It is wiser to spend money on publicity and Web sites than buying expensive office space.

Question: What are the biggest mistakes new consultants make when marketing themselves?

Response: Spending money on brochures is a huge mistake because they are outdated the moment you pick one up. You feel compelled to send them out and the recipient ends up throwing it in the wastebasket. It's a huge waste of paper. I don't think you should rely on just the Internet.

I think mail is still valuable and direct marketing can still have a great impact because people are using e-mail so much. You need to use a mix of marketing tools to create a buzz and not rely on the Internet. I have heard people say they used to use a newsletter and it worked well, but they discontinued doing it because of the cost and time. On the other hand, if you use a newsletter as an educational tool, customers will feel they are getting value.

Question: What is the cleverest idea you have heard a consultant use to build visibility?

Response: A business associate of mine had a client that started an office-cleaning business. She used a series of postcards to attract clients. The first card said, "Naturally we brush daily,"and the second card read, "We want to be your main squeegee." It was very successful. You really need to get your name and image in front of people six times for someone to remember you.

Question: How long does it usually take for marketing campaigns to yield results?

Response: It usually takes three months to a year. If not, you need to change consultants or reevaluate what you are doing.

Question: What is the one piece of advice you would give a consultant about marketing him- or herself?

Response: You need to build your database from the first day you start your business. I would recommend endorsement marketing. Get your clients to write endorsement letters on their letterhead and ask them if you could send those letters out to prospects in your database. Also ask them if they are willing to send those letters to companies they do business with. You, however, will need to pay for the mailings. I once had a client who sent out 60 of my books, which yielded seven strong leads.

Making the Plan Real

Now that you know which tools to use and what one successful consultant recommends, you need to develop two other plans:

Launch Plan. I have seen countless new consultants run around like chickens with their heads cut off buying business cards, stationery, joining trade associations, putting up Web sites, and trying to get new business all at one time and complaining that nothing is coming out right and feeling disorganized. Take the time to make a list of all the tasks you need to do and decide on reasonable deadlines for getting those things done. Once you do that, you can put together a marketing budget.

Month 1

Engage marketing firm
Design company image (product, Web site, marketing materials)
Develop marketing materials (mailer, Web site, e-mail)
Develop and launch phase 1 of the Web site
Engage hosting service

Month 2

Develop and launch phase 2 of the Web site
Hire public relations firm
Run two advertisements in industry magazines

Month 3

Develop and launch phase 3 of the Web site

Run three advertisements in industry magazines

Month 4

Run four advertisements in industry magazines

Month 5

Run five advertisements in industry magazines

Month 6

Run six advertisements in industry magazines
Attend trade show

Month 7

Run seven advertisements in industry magazines

Month 8

Run eight advertisements in industry magazines
Send a direct mail piece to potential resellers
Send e-mail to potential resellers and end-users

Month 9

Run nine advertisements in industry magazines
Attend trade show

Month 10

Run 10 advertisements in industry magazines

Month 11

Run advertisements in industry magazines
Attend trade show

Month 12

Run advertisements in industry magazines

Marketing Budget. Once you have determined what industries you are going after, whom you need to contact, how you plan to reach them, and a time frame in which to accomplish everything, you need to put together a marketing budget. This will help you plan out your cash flow and narrow your choices of what you plan to do and when you plan to do it.

Categories	Year 1	Year 2	Year 3	Year 4	Year 5
Total Marketing Support	$81,690	$122,255	$137,393	$153,116	$171,146
Direct Mail (Postcards)	$225	$1,890	$2,333	$2,929	$3,639
No. of Letters	1,500	1,800	2,160	2,592	3,110
Cost per Mailing	0	0	0	0	0
Cost per Name	0	0	0	0	0
Cost per Letter	$1	$1	$1	$1	$1
Collateral and Printing	$2,650	$5,600	$8,700	$12,200	$16,250
Envelopes	1	1	1	1	1
Stationery	0	0	0	0	0
No. of Each Piece	5,000	10,000	15,000	20,000	25,000
Advertising and PR Agency	$30,000	$30,000	$36,000	$41,400	$47,610
No. of Months	10	10	10	10	10
Cost per Month	$3,000	$3,000	$3,600	$4,140	$4,761
Seminars	$4,000	$4,400	$4,840	$5,324	$5,856
No. of Seminars	2	2	2	2	2
Cost per Show	$2,000	$2,200	$2,420	$2,662	$2,928
Roundtables	$4,000	$4,400	$7,260	$7,986	$8,784
No. of Roundtables	4	4	6	6	6
Average Cost per Roundtable	$1,000	$1,100	$1,210	$1,331	$1,464

FIGURE 6-1. Marketing budget (Continued on page 110)

Newsletter	$6,400	$6,720	$7,056	$7,408	$7,780
Frequency	4	4	4	4	4
Cost for Printing	$1,600	$1,680	$1,764	$1,852	$1,945
Editor	$1,000	$1,050	$1,103	$1,158	$1,216
Direct E-mail	$600	$1,350	$2,025	$3,038	$4,556
No. of E-mails	1,500	2,250	3,375	5,063	7,594
Cost per Name	$0.20	$0.20	$0.20	$0.20	$0.20
Number of Mailings	2	3	3	3	3
Book	$30,000	$20,500	$21,025	$21,576	$22,155
Cost for Writer	$10,000	0	0	0	0
Cost to Publish	$10,000	$10,000	$10,000	$10,000	$10,000
No. of Books	2,000	2,000	2,000	2,000	2,000
Cost per Book	$5	$5.25	$5.51	$5.79	$6.08
Cost to Mail	$3,000	$3,200	$3,400	$3,400	$3,600
No. of Books	2,000	2,000	2,000	2,000	2,000
Cost for Mailing	$1.50	$1.60	$1.70	$1.70	$1.80

FIGURE 6-1. Marketing budget (Continued)

Chapter Key Points

One of the keys to building a successful consulting practice is to develop an executable and affordable marketing plan. Do the following and you will create visibility and buzz about your services:

🔑 Planning—Take the time to plan your marketing attack and bounce it off colleagues and friends.

🔑 Identify targets—Identify industry and position targets within industries.

🔑 Tools—Talk with trade association professionals in the industry you are targeting and find out which marketing tools will have the greatest effect.

Execute—Whether you do it yourself or hire someone, make sure your marketing plan is executed professionally.

Don't look at marketing as a frivolous expense. How many successful businesses are you aware of that aren't good at marketing themselves?

ON-LINE MARKETING

THE INTERNET IS YOUR FRIEND ◄

Seven or eight years ago, having a Web site was a novelty, and if you could find a computer programmer or graphic artist who could develop one you were lucky. Five years ago, multimedia companies who were developing CD-ROMs began to realize that the Internet would quickly displace the CD-ROM as the mass-marketing vehicle of choice so they learned to develop Web sites. Advertising agency executives were hearing from their younger associates that they needed to be able to develop Web sites or lose major advertising customers.

According to the Gartner Group, a nationally respected research firm, 80 percent of small businesses will have a Web presence by 2004, and between 50 and 60 percent currently have Web sites. Potential Web-site developers include:

- advertising agencies
- printers or graphics houses
- computer-programming firms
- software developers
- multimedia companies
- local newspapers
- Internet service providers (ISPs)
- Web-site development firms
- on-line services (www.homestead.com)
- independent/part-time Web developers

You should do two things before contacting a Web developer or developing the site yourself. The first is to buy a domain name. You can do this by going to various domain resellers, such as All-Domains (www.alldomains.com) and Register.com (www.register.com). The second thing you must do is decide what type of information should be found on your Web site and whether you plan to use technology such as streaming media, PDF files, or on-line surveys. Your plan should focus on the following areas:

- **Mission:** What is the purpose of the Web site? Is it to build sales and marketing momentum, improve client service, or both?
- **Functionality:** Are you selling your services over the Internet? Do you want to have multimedia capability and add sound and pictures?
- **User Reward:** What kind of information is going to be on the site that will bring users back? Will you be changing the content daily, weekly, monthly, quar-

> *Nothing frustrates people more than long download times. Make your functionality simple and intuitive.*

> *A friend of mine has a three-person company specializing in small Web sites that take less than six weeks to put together. They can develop simple databases and take an off-the-shelf electronic commerce package and integrate it into your Web site.*

terly, or yearly? Who will be responsible?

- **Owner Benefit:** Are you looking to attract new customers? Create brand awareness?

Once the plan is written, you need to decide how much money you are willing to spend.

It has been my experience that you can save a lot of time and heartache by telling developers the budget for the project. Many businesses are reluctant to do this for fear that they will overpay or find out later that they could have gotten more for their money.

Large national and regional Web-site developers really can't afford to take on projects that cost less than $100,000. There are exceptions to the rule, but large developers excel at building big Web sites with lots of functionality and database connectivity.

After almost four years of real consumer and business awareness, many Web-site developers now have a body of work and, in many cases, a niche industry they excel at or have developed well, for example, electronic commerce solutions or building and integrating back-end databases and great graphics.

Finding a Web-Site Developer

The best, easiest, and most efficient way to select a Web-site developer is to follow these steps:

Step 1:

- Look at the companies in your region whose Web sites you admire and find out who developed them.
- Look at competitor Web sites and see who developed those.
- Look at the sites that have the types of functionality you would like and see who is developing those.

Step 2: Develop a request for proposal that asks each developer for a list of the sites he or she has developed, the number of full-time employees he or she has, and a breakdown of full-time project managers, graphic designers, and programmers, including the specialty of each programmer. If the body of work is with business-to-consumer companies and you are business-to-business, the fit may not be right. If your business is complicated, like pharmaceuticals or money management, you may want a company that understands your industry.

Step 3: Don't ask for references; contact the companies for which the developer has developed sites. Ask those companies if the developer is good at meeting deadlines, flexible concerning changes, able to come up with ideas independently, and willing to provide additional services that the company didn't have to pay for. For example, did the developer suggest unsolicited ideas for improving the site? Did the developer send articles related to the client's business or the state of the Internet industry?

Step 4: Once you begin talking to developers, find out whether your money will attract experienced talent or only a junior person who is going to cut his or her teeth on your project. Ask for the list of projects the project manager and team have worked on and for their site-development methodology. Ask to see a sample site map and development flow chart they have developed for other clients.

Step 5: If this is your first Web site, find a local firm whose developers are within driving distance of your office. You will find you will want to inspect their offices and visit with them during the development of the project. Don't worry about their hourly rate: just make sure they understand your business and can develop your project within the budget and time you have given them.

All too often, consultancies make the mistake of calling in Web-site developers and handing them a simple description of what they want. Many of my clients believe that, if they show an experienced developer one or more Web sites that match their concept, the developer will be able to give them a price. You need to develop a plan of your own.

Four Steps to Developing a Successful Web-Site Plan

There are four steps to developing a good Web-site plan:

1. Decide who will be responsible day to day for the Web site.
2. Develop a request for proposal.
3. Develop criteria and a list of developers to interview.
4. Develop a list of hosting services to interview.

I interviewed Robin Niefield, a marketing veteran who launched her Internet career in 1994 with the development of one of the Web's first affiliate networks. In 1996, Robin cofounded NetPlus Marketing, Inc., an on-line advertising and marketing agency that serves clients such as AstraZeneca Pharmaceuticals, David's Bridal, Toll Brothers, Sun Microsystems, Mars Music, Atofina Chemicals, Philly.com, Jobnet, and others. Under her leadership, NetPlus Marketing has enjoyed solid, continuous growth by providing best-of-breed, results-driven services. She is a frequent speaker at industry events across the country, including ClickZ and Thunderlizard, and is often sought after for her insight, advice, and comments from industry and business publications. Robin holds a B.A. from Wellesley College and an M.B.A. from the University of Chicago.

Question: Should you develop the site yourself or have a professional do it?

Response: For the same reasons that you hire experts and you promote your expertise to clients, you should have someone expert in Web-site development involved in your project. The key is to collaboratively plan your site, clearly defining the site objectives and cataloging your resources to maintain and update the site after it is launched. Work together to make sure that the final product reflects your voice, offerings, and needs.

Question: How many pages should a consultant's site be?

Response: Start small. Overly ambitious Web-site projects tend to bog down, particularly in the planning stages and in the content-collection efforts. You should initially include the features, content, and functionality required to meet your primary Web-site objectives, understanding that a Web site is never a discrete project with a beginning and an end. Your site should change over time as it reflects changes in the industry, environment, technology, and your business.

Think in terms of phases. If you are watching your traffic trends, your site registrations, and other relevant metrics, you will have a good picture of what your audience is finding valuable and what is driving your results. That information is critical in guiding Phase II and later development efforts.

Question: What information should you have on the site?

Response: Every Web site should integrate contact information into the page design so that it is up-front and visible on each and every page. Professional service firms have a specific need to establish credibility on-line. Think about what qualifying questions prospects ask you and work to address those issues in the content of your site. Client lists and testimonials, speaking engagements, published works, case studies, and sample deliverables are all good credibility enhancers.

Question: What should you expect to spend if you hire an outside firm or person to develop your site?

Response: There are lots of options available at all budget and skill levels. Interview several and check references. Visit the sites they have done. Note whether they ask key questions like:

- What can you tell me about your business/industry/clients?
- Who are you trying to reach with this Web site?
- What are your objectives with the Web site?
- Do you anticipate maintaining and updating the content yourself?
- What kind of personnel and resources will be assigned to your Web-site efforts? What relevant skills do they have?
- Do you plan to promote the Web site to increase targeted traffic?
- Do you plan to use the Web site to service your clients or deliver work product? How?
- What would make this site a successful complement to your other marketing efforts?
- What metrics will be important to your evaluation of this effort?

Question: Should you develop a plan of what you want on the site?

Response: Absolutely. It would be akin to handing a builder a hammer and some lumber and telling him to build a building. You need an architect to draft the plan, in this case an information architect who understands your business and your goals.

Question: Should you ask clients and potential clients what types of information they would like to see?

Response: The best source of information is going to be the objective data that you get from your Web site. In advance of your first site efforts, you should query your own staff. Ask those staff members with client and prospect contact what questions they are routinely asked. What are the critical information items that get them to the next step with your prospects? Visit competitor and industry sites to get a sense of the expectations in the industry.

Question: Should the colors on the site match your marketing materials?

Response: Yes, but it goes much further than just making sure the look and feel is consistent. Integrate all your marketing efforts so that they support a common objective but make the best possible use of each medium's strength. The strength of the Internet is the ability to create an interactive experience and a two-way dialogue with your customers and prospects.

Question: What types of information create "stickiness" for consultants?

Response: Tools and calculators, lists of resources, on-line newsletters, anything that your market is going to find valuable and would not or could not easily produce for themselves. The trick is to change the content to give users a reason to return to the site multiple times, perhaps regularly. A common tactic is to post news or information on the site and send e-mail updates that link back to the site, thus driving repeat visits.

Question: What are the most common mistakes service firms make when developing a Web site?

> *One of my clients spent a lot of money on developing a game to show the company had a fun side. When I interviewed my client's clients, they were unimpressed and wondered why my client wasted space on the site with information that wasn't helpful to them.*

Response: Internet newbies often throw up an on-line brochure, commonly called brochureware, or use a templated quickie solution that recites critical information about the firm but does not take advantage of the unique and interactive nature of the Web. It is better to start small but work smart. You can build your site over time into an interactive powerhouse that supports your business objectives.

Web-Site Leader

Someone has to be responsible on a day-to-day basis for the Web site. For someone just starting a consulting practice, you might ask your developer to do this or outsource the task to your spouse or significant other if he or she has the following skills:

- the ability make decisions about content;
- expertise in marketing;
- understanding of your company's overall strategic business goals;
- understanding of what your customers would find valuable.

Developing a Request for Proposal

Before you launch your Web site, make sure you understand how long and how much it will cost to build a quality Web site that you can add on to and won't have to scrap after one year. I had an international client who hired one of the largest Web-site development companies in the world, but they hadn't developed a plan to give the developers that mapped out exactly what information they wanted to give to prospects and customers and how that information would be extracted and integrated with their current information systems.

By the time the project was complete—to the tune of $25,000—the president of the company fired the developer and had to spend money on a new developer. He realized the site was a failure when customers called and wrote to him about problems accessing important information and the difficulty in navigating the site. He then had his outsourced CIO and public relations consultant work together with me and outside developers to develop a new plan. The new site, which was much more robust and user-friendly than the old site, will cost almost half of what the old site cost to develop.

Elements of a Proposal

Don't delude yourself into thinking that your plan will be perfect. Developing a proposal to give to developers is a great first step. It provides insight into what you think you want and need. Good developers will be able to take your plan and provide feedback that will improve your site and, possibly, save you money.

A good proposal contains the following parts:

- **Mission.** The mission of your Web site should describe what your company and the user will get out of the site. The mission of Dell Computer's Web site is to allow buyers to save time and money by building their own computer. The value to Dell is that they develop a one-on-one relationship with the buyer and they don't have to build computers that may not meet the customer's needs.

- **Content.** What type of information will the user find on the site? Content will range from basic company information to descriptions of products and services to press releases to white papers about the company's industry.

- **User description.** The developers need to know if the end user is a consumer with a traditional 28.8 or 56K modem, or a corporate user with high-speed access. This will give the developer insight into the type of graphics and audio- and video-streaming technology the user will be able to access.

- **Site technology.** All site content is written in word-processing or text editor software and converted to HTML or XML. Professional developers use Go Live and Macromedia's Web-authoring tools. Developers need to know whether there will there be databases to which users will have access. Will those databases be accessible to everyone or will they be password-protected? What database program was used to develop those databases and are all the databases developed in one common language? Do you plan to use video- and audio-streaming, and how many people do you anticipate will be using video and audio simultaneously? The developers need to know all of this to determine what type of professionals to include in the site's development team.

- **Internal technology.** Developers need to know the type of hardware and operating systems on which your databases and content reside in case they have to extract information or build links to information that resides on internal computers. They also need to know if you plan to host your Web site internally or outsource it.

- **Site map.** Two types of site maps must be developed. One is a spreadsheet that includes names for each section and subsection, descriptions of each section, and the type of software and technology required to access the information for each section. The developers need to know who, on the client's team, is responsible for what. Finally, the developers need to know how many pages are projected for each section and subsection.

The other site map looks like an architectural plan. It includes boxes with the names of each section and subsection mentioned in the spreadsheet site-map plan, and arrows between the boxes indicating how the sections and subsections are to be linked to one another.

Sample Proposal

The proposal you develop should be labeled "Draft." It will be a draft because you will be revising the information in the plan based on the discussions, feedback, and questions you get from developers. Below is a sample request for proposal for Web-site developers to review:

Kadoch Marketing Request for Proposal

Contact Person: Marc Kramer, 610-873-6978, marc@kramercommunications.com

Description of the Company: Kadoch Marketing develops and implements business and marketing plans for financial institutions.

Budget: The budget is not to exceed $15,000.

Operating Environment: The principals of the company operate out of their homes and will not be hosting the site. The site will be made up mostly of static pages, with the exception of on-line calculators and links to Amazon.com to sell business books.

Technical Requirement: An overview of the type of information we will supply to Web-site developers is shown below. The focus will be to develop a graphically inviting home page that is quickly downloaded and uses off-the-shelf products for electronic commerce, customer service, and security.

Site Plan:

Section	Content	Work Ownership	Pgs
About Company	Information about our mission/ objectives	Internally developed word doc-links	1
Management	Name, title, bio, telephone, e-mail	Internally developed word doc-links	1
Fees	Description of fees	Internally developed word doc	1
Sample Projects	Sample business and marketing plans	Internally developed word doc	1
Reference List	Past client contact information	Internally developed word doc	1
Clients by Industry			
Banking	Name of client and description of project	Internally developed word doc	2
Insurance	Name of client and description of project	Internally developed word doc	2
Money Management	Name of client and description of project	Internally developed word doc	2
Venture Capital	Name of client and description of project	Internally developed word doc	2
Products			
Book Reviews	Promote books by focus (consulting, etc.)	Information supplied by publishers	2
New Products	One-paragraph descriptions of new products	Information supplied by manufacturers	1
Technology	One-page checklist of products needed to start biz	Links to our partners to sell products	1
Success Stories			
Success Stories	Client success stories	Internally developed word doc	1
Financing Sources			
Angel Capital	Explanation of funding source and expert interview	Link to funding source partners	2
Bank Capital	Explanation of funding source and expert interview	Link to funding source partners	2
Corporate Venture Capital	Explanation of funding source and expert interview	Link to funding source partners	2

Government Capital	Explanation of funding source and expert interview	Link to funding source partners	2
Factoring	Explanation of funding source and expert interview	Link to funding source partners	2
Venture Capital	Explanation of funding source and expert interview	Link to funding source partners	2
Tools			
Business Plan Wizard	Description of our Business Plan Wizard	Link to Wizard	1
Calculators	Description of the various calculators	Link to Thebancorp's calculators	1
Total Pages			32

Building Your Own Site

If you have the computer skills, a good eye for design, and the necessary time, you can develop your own site. There are a few services and products that will help you.

Services: The following are on-line services that provide you with either the tools or the templates to build your own Web site. The templates are different designs you can choose from and input your information.

- ZyWeb (www.zy.com)
- Homestead (www.homestead.com)
- VeriSign (www.verisign.com)

Software: Any office supply super store will have software that will allow you to build your own Web site. The following are a few products you may want to look at:

- Adobe WebCollection (www.adobe.com)
- Microsoft Front Page (www.microsoft.com)
- WebEasy (www.v-com.com)

For basic, static sites these products work fine.

Signing Up with Search Engines

If you want to generate business from your Web site, you need to do two things. First, you have to make sure that whoever develops your Web site has written key words into the code that will alert a search engine about the content in your site. Second, you need to sign up with the various search engines. Most people only know of Altavista, AOL Search, AskJeeves, Direct Hit, Excite, InfoSeek, Yahoo, Excite, Google, and Dogpile. Numerous services will automatically sign you up with the various search engines, but the easiest may be to use whomever you bought and registered your domain name with.

A great site to get an understanding of how search engines work and how to sign up for them is Search Engine Watch (www.search-enginewatch.com).

Hosting Charges

Once you have your site built, you need a company to host it on a computer so people can see your site. According to Yahoo, there are over 4,500 companies that host Web sites. I use a company that is local to my area called Bee Net (www.bee.net), whose chart is displayed below. This chart and its services are typical of what most hosting services offer. I recommend using a small local service as opposed to a national service, because a small one will provide more personalized service, and the prices in many cases are better because the smaller services have lower overhead costs.

Pay Period	Value Package	Most Popular Package
	Perfect for brochure-type Web sites	Includes Web-site statistics, FrontPage, ASP, and ODBC
Monthly	$40	$50
Quarterly	$110	$140
Yearly	$400	$500
One-time setup fee	$50	$75

Web Site Hosting and Maintenance	Value Package	Most Popular Package
Registration or transfer of domain name	Yes	Yes
Registration service provider fee for registration of new domain name. Includes use of domain name on the Internet for one year.	$20	$20
Windows NT 4.0/IIS 4.0 server hosting	Yes	Yes
Password-protected unlimited 24/7 FTP access for editing site, using any Internet access account	Yes	Yes
Web site storage space	20 MB	50 MB
Monthly bandwidth allowance	2 GB	5 GB
E-Mail Features		
Number of separate e-mail accounts	4	4
Additional e-mail boxes (no setup fee for additional boxes added at startup)	$10 setup fee plus $5/month, $15/quarter, or $50/year	$10 setup fee plus $5/month, $15/quarter, or $50/year
Unlimited incoming e-mail aliases via wildcard alias *@domainname.com	Yes	Yes
Mail forwarding option	Yes	Yes
Access e-mail from non-Bee.Net Internet access account via any Internet mail software	Yes	Yes
Web browser-based e-mail account administration	Yes	Yes
E-mail auto-responder feature	Yes	Yes

Web Site Marketing Features	Value Package	Most Popular Package
Homepage counter cgi	Yes	Yes
Listing in Bee.Net Gallery	Yes	Yes
Webtrends Web-site statistics: www.domainname.com/stats	—	Updated monthly
Web-Site Developer Product Support (on request)		
Form to e-mail processing using Formalis WebFormLite for single forms or Formalis WebForm for multiple forms	Yes	Yes
Microsoft FrontPage 2000 server extensions	—	Yes
Allaire Cold Fusion 4.x tag support	—	Yes
ASP (Microsoft Active Server Pages) support	—	Yes
MDAC 2.x and ODBC database-connector support (including MS Access 97 and 2000)	—	Yes
CDONT/SMTP support	—	Yes
PHP Hypertext Preprocessor support	—	Yes
Optional Services		
Additional storage space	$10/10 MB/month	
Additional bandwidth	$10/100 MB/month	
VeriSign SSL encryption for form processing, using Bee.Net certificate	$25 setup fee plus $20/month, $55/quarter, or $200/year	
VeriSign SSL encryption for form processing, using your own certificate: $349 initial and $249 annual fees paid to VeriSign	$50 setup fee plus $20/month, $55/quarter, or $200/year	
Microsoft Visual Basic 6 cgi support	$25 setup fee plus $20/month, $55/quarter, or $200/year	

Optional Services	Value Package	Most Popular Package
Microsoft SQL Server 7x support (includes 30 MB database space)	$50 setup fee plus $25/month, $70/quarter, or $250/year	
Additional domain name pointing to same content	$50 setup fee plus $20/month, $55/quarter, or $200/year	
Hypermedia ECware shopping cart (fees include SSL, setup of Web-server environment, and license to use software on Bee.Net's server)	$500 setup fee plus $40/month, $110/quarter, or $400/year	
Add Dial-up Internet Access		
Modem or v.90 Internet access, interactive use only, pricing per user. This discounted pricing is available if the related services are included in the same billing and payment as the Web site.	$20 setup fee plus $17/month	
ISDN Internet access, interactive use only, pricing per user (does not include Verizon fees)	$20 setup fee plus $34.95/month, $99/quarter, or $370/year	

Chapter Key Points

The importance of preplanning your Web site and taking the time to find the right developer can't be stressed enough. Smart planning involves listing the following requirements:

- appropriate and sufficient content;
- amount of and provisions for interactivity;
- identifying the person internally responsible for providing content;
- specifying which parts of the site will be linked to other parts of the site;
- ordered priorities for the developers.

During the development process, don't make changes constantly, because it will frustrate everyone involved. Once the site is up, reevaluate it and make changes.

HOW TO FIND CLIENTS

MAKING CONTACTS WITH THOSE WHO NEED HELP ◄

Т*he easiest part of being a consultant is doing the work. The two hardest parts are getting contracts and collecting your fees. Before you can collect fees, however, you need to develop clients. Fortunately, I have been able to develop an extensive contact base because I run a large trade association, write books and newspaper columns, and sit on the boards of companies and nonprofit organizations.*

In Chapters 5 and 6, I wrote about how to build visibility so people will know who you are, what you do, and that, at some point, they will be hearing from you. Most consultants I have met love their work, but hate having to pitch their services. In order to make this necessary self-promotion less unpleasant, the following sections will describe ways to increase your visibility:

- *Selecting and Leveraging Membership Organizations*
- *Professionals to Target*
- *On-line Services to Join*
- *On-line Referral Services*
- *Sales Lead Lists*
- *National, State, and Regional Organizations to Join*
- *Trade Shows to Attend*

Selecting and Leveraging Membership Organizations

Half of my new clients come from relationships I have made through organizations I belong to. Don't join organizations only for the sake of meeting people. Select organizations by the type of contacts you can make. Always remember that you are selling your time and can't afford to waste it on organizations that won't provide the appropriate contacts.

When I started my consulting practice, I developed criteria for the type of organizations I wanted to join. Organizations must have the following attributes to get me to write a check:

1. **Business Focus.** I look at which industries or type of people the organization serves. If you provide marketing services to attorneys, then you want to join your county or city chapter of the American Bar Association.

2. **Organizational Level of Members.** I typically target the highest level in an organization, from vice president to CEO. In my case, these are the people who typically contract for my services. If you provide interior-design consulting, you probably won't target that high a level. You are probably looking for office and building managers. Talking to the president might be a complete waste of time.

3. **Average Revenue of Members.** Most successful consultants follow a simple rule: Don't take on clients who have less cash than you do. Every time I have taken on a client who I sensed had less money than I did or who asked me to break up payments, I have gotten burned. I typically look for clients who have a minimum of $1 million in annual revenue or $500,000 in invested capital.

4. **Ability to Meet Check Signers.** I always want to meet

No Clout

Nothing is more frustrating than meeting someone who gets excited about what you do, which, in turn, gets you pumped up, only to find out that he or she doesn't have the authority to hire you and little clout in the organization to influence retaining you. Ask up front what the person does before scheduling a meeting to make sure he or she can either write the check or influence the individual who does write the check.

people who can write me a check. I am not interested in meeting someone from an organization who likes what I do, but has no real power or influence.

5. **Ability to Meet Client Influencers.** Influencers come in many shapes and sizes. Some are internal to a company and some are outside of a company, for example, advisory board members, accountants, attorneys, and information-systems professionals. Three-quarters of my referrals and introductions come from influencers. Most times prospective clients won't even ask for references if someone they trust made the introduction.

6. **Opportunity to Speak at Seminars.** Speaking is one of the great ways to develop credibility and attract clients. Anytime I have ever spoken, people have come up to me afterwards and asked for my business card and to meet with me to discuss working with them. People automatically assume that, if you have been asked to speak, you are an expert, and everyone wants to talk with and hire the expert.

7. **Opportunity to Write for Organizational Publications.** Most organizations have either a print or an on-line publication. Like speaking engagements, writing articles builds a lot of credibility. See if the organization allows and encourages its members to write. Writing doesn't bring in prospects like speaking does, but it

does give you credibility and something to send to prospective clients as a way of reminding them about who you are and how much value you bring.

8. **Opportunity to Serve on Organization Board.** It's rare that a person can just join an organization and be selected to the board of directors. As with any organization you join, you want to know if it has advisory or sub-boards that will allow you to develop relationships with your target market or influencers. If they don't and it takes you years to get on a panel, then you might have to reconsider the value of the organization.

9. **Quality of Membership Directory.** Notice that this is almost at the bottom of my list. I have never received a telephone call from anyone who has looked in a membership directory and called me. The value of the directory is to learn about other members. I look for directories that have the full range of useful information, such as:
   - description of the company
   - description of the core product/service
   - list of key executives
   - street address
   - telephone numbers
   - fax number
   - e-mail address
   - Web site address

   There are many organizations that don't provide either a paper directory or a password-protected on-line directory.

10. **Cost to Join the Organization.** Most people look at the cost of joining an organization first and then decide if they are going to join. If the cost is $100 a year to join, most people think they have little to lose because it is so cheap to join. On the other hand, if they have to pay $500 or more, they will look at the price and come up

---

The Perfect Membership Organization

I joined an organization in the Philadelphia area called the Entrepreneurs' Forum of Greater Philadelphia. The organization's mission is to educate would-be entrepreneurs. The board is made up of entrepreneurs and individuals who service them, such as accountants, lawyers, investment bankers, commercial bankers, and executive recruiters. Membership is free to anyone, but to be a sponsor and join the board you have to pay $500. You can't imagine how hard it is to get people to write a $500 check.

This organization met every one of my 10 criteria. In the past two years, I have signed four clients, who have paid me a total of $35,000. Would you trade $1,500 over three years for $35,000? Surprisingly, many people have passed on that opportunity.

Before you join any organization, take a look at the profile of your target influencer and target buyer that you developed as part of your marketing plan.

---

with reasons why the organization isn't worth joining. My rule of thumb regarding price is, if I can pick up one client within two years, that will justify paying the membership.

Professionals to Target

Every industry has a group of professionals to target and you need to make a list of who those targets are so you know whom to speak to. Just as you developed a list of criteria for the organizations you join, you should develop one for the professionals you plan to target. You don't want to waste time with people who can't pay you or can't lead you to people who can pay you.

I developed four criteria for determining which professionals I should target:

1. **Industry Representation:** In the 1990s, information technology consultants were telling everyone that they were industry-independent. When there is huge

demand and limited supply for a particular service, that often holds true, but for most of business history people hired individuals because of their expertise in a field. My areas of expertise are financial, certain areas of technology and software, and acquiring venture capital for Internet startups.

2. **Level in Management:** Associations exist for every level of management. In the early 1990s, when I was running a trade association, my office manager took me to a meeting of office managers in the Philadelphia area where the speaker was CEO of the 20th-largest bank in the United States. Why was the CEO of the 20th-largest bank speaking to office managers? Because many office managers in small businesses are responsible for banking activities. If you were selling services that office managers buy, such as travel, computer services, payroll, and so forth, you would want to join that group.

3. **Departmental:** Because I am typically retained by marketing and salespeople, I look for organizations that focus on those departments or have subgroups focused on those departments. In my practice, small-town and rural county chambers of commerce offer me little opportunity. Large chambers, such as the Greater Philadelphia Chamber of Commerce, which has thousands of companies of all sizes as members, caters to a variety of professionals and, therefore, offers me great opportunities.

4. **Size of Company:** A few of the consultants I interviewed for this book needed global or national clients because their fees are $300 an hour and they typically require $5,000 per month for a minimum of six months. There aren't a lot of companies under $10 million that are willing to allocate $60,000 for various projects.

Never forget that you are selling your time, and lost time costs you money, literally; therefore, be selective about which groups you join. Various types of consultants and the people they target are shown below:

Type of Consultant	Check-Writer Target	Influencer Target
Marketing	Vice President of Marketing Marketing Director Brand Manager	President Investment Banker Commercial Banker
Interior Design	Homeowners Presidents of Companies	Architects General Contractors Building Contractors
Finance Experts	Presidents of Companies Chief Financial Officers Treasurers	Accountants Lawyers Advisory Board Members
Speech Coach	Presidents of Companies Director of Communications Human Resource Professionals	Advertising Executives Public Relations Professionals Outside Human Resource Professionals
Evaluation Experts	Presidents of Companies Chief Financial Officers Outside Investors	Commercial Banker Investment Banker Outside Board of Directors

On-Line Services to Join

People are still making jokes about the swan dive the Internet sector took starting in the spring of 2000. Anyone who has studied business history was not surprised by what happened. In the beginning of the automotive age, there were over 120 car manufacturers and the same can be said of the computer and biotechnology industries. The Internet is alive and still growing throughout the world.

A number of on-line services are focused on helping consultants attract new opportunities. All of the services I am listing have been around for at least a couple of years and some for as long as four years. They provide buyers of services with easy-to-use interfaces and give sellers of services a chance to attract new clients from around the globe.

How does it work? Either the on-line referral services charge a per-sales lead fee, which means the seller of services pays a fee to respond to requests for proposals, or the seller of services pays a percentage of the contract to the provider of sales leads.

On-Line Referral Services

The following services have been around the longest and focus on providing sales leads to consultants:

- www.elance.com
- www.rfpmarket.com
- www.soho.org

Check with your regional daily newspapers and chambers of commerce to see if they have licensed or co-branded these services to attract readers and members and create regional business activity.

Sales Lead Lists

Buying mailing lists makes sense if you have an unusual service to offer or you want to build visibility for your service. Here are the best places to buy or rent lists:

- **American Business Journals** (www.bizjournals.com): This is a business newspaper chain that has created directories for each of the more than 20 cities it is in. The directories usually list the Top 25 to 150 companies and organizations, ranging from Accounting to Banking to Public Companies to Venture Capital. You can buy either a paper version or the lists on CD-ROM or diskette. Each list contains the name of the company, business leader, address, telephone, fax, and Web-site address.

- **American List Council** (www.amlist.com): ALC sells mailing lists and databases owned by other companies. You never actually buy a mailing list; you can only rent them. You can rent them to use for a one-time mailing and, in some cases, the seller will let you rent the list for continual use for one year.

- **Dun & Bradstreet** (www.dnb.com): This organization has the largest business database in the world. It can provide the name of a company, the company leader or leaders, address, telephone, and fax numbers. As I am writing this book, D&B provides few Web-site addresses and no e-mail addresses.

- **InfoUSA** (www.infousa.com): You can buy information by region, state, or the entire country on CD-ROM. This service provides name of company, company leader, address, telephone, fax, and, in some cases, e-mail and Web-site addresses. You usually can find these CD-ROMs in office supply stores such as Staples, Office Max, and Office Depot.

Finally, every chamber of commerce and business organization that has full-time support staff provides paper and on-line directories. My advice is to join local organizations and start by using their directories. By joining the organization, you have a reason to write to fellow members.

Regardless of which lists you use, you need to send a concise letter or e-mail, which allows for easy follow-up and conversation. The following is a sample communication I use:

*B*efore you buy any list, find out how often the list is updated and whether old addresses are periodically removed. Avoid buying lists that are only scrubbed once every other year or longer. Also, make sure the list has contact names, addresses, telephone numbers, and, most importantly, e-mail addresses, which is the form of communication most people prefer today.

Dear Mr. Johnson:

I recently joined the Chester County Chamber of Commerce. I noticed that your company is also a member and read the description about your company in the membership directory. The reason for my correspondence is that I noticed that you don't have a marketing director and I provide out-source marketing services.

Prior to starting my consulting practice, I was the chief marketing officer for Kramer Medical Equipment and Victory Candy & Tobacco. I develop and implement marketing plans, which means I work with management to create the strategy and then I take responsibility for implementing the strategy, which includes:

- Developing copy for brochures and evaluating and selecting vendors
- Developing and implementing marketing partnerships
- Developing and implementing speaking opportunities

If you would like to know more about me, please go to my Web site (www.kramercommunications.com). I will call your office within the week to inquire whether you have time to see me at the office or to meet for breakfast or lunch. Have a great day.

Sincerely,

Marc Kramer

President

National, State, and Regional Organizations to Join

Practically everyone I have ever come across in business has belonged to some type of business organization. Much to my surprise, many people who have made a career of working for *Fortune* 1000 companies have rarely been involved with outside membership organizations because their company wouldn't pay for it or the person didn't see the need to spend his or her own money to join. You can't get business if you don't join organizations.

There are organizations for everyone to join, ranging from specific industries, such as the Biotechnology Industry Organization (www.bio.org), which works with biotechnology and pharmaceutical companies and individuals who sell products and services to them, to the National Venture Capital Association (www.nvca.org), which caters to venture capitalists.

How do you find these organizations? Ways to find the right organization for you include:

- **National Trade Associations:** There is an organization that every trade association joins, the American Society of Association Executives (www. asaenet.org). You can either find links or contact ASAE to find organizations that fit your focus. You can also go to the Small Business Administration Web site (www.sba.gov), which has links to national organizations as well.

- **State and Regional Organizations:** Every state in the United States has a Web site and every state has a Department of Commerce to attract and stimulate business. Go to your state's Web site and you will find links to state and regional organizations to join.

- **Media:** Many regional newspapers, radio, and television station Web sites provide links to regional organizations. If you go to one of the search engines and type in the type of organization you are looking for and the state you are in, you can find links to organizations.

Trade Shows to Attend

It has been my experience that trade shows are a great way to make contacts that will lead to business. There are two types of trade show: regional and industry. To find out about these shows, go to one of the following sources:

- national and regional publications
- regional convention centers
- state and regional chambers of commerce
- state and regional tourist bureaus

I interviewed Bruce Polkes, President of The Benchview Group and former product brand manager for Procter & Gamble and Aloette Foods, about the best ways of finding new clients. He has an undergraduate degree in engineering from Johns Hopkins University and an M.B.A. from Northwestern University Kellogg School of Management. His business is focused on developing and implementing marketing plans for companies at every stage of development. He doesn't encourage startup consulting practices to pour large amounts of money into consulting. He is a true believer in guerrilla marketing.

Question: What is the most effective way to market a new consulting business?

Response: In a word: contacts! Go for the low-hanging fruit first. Using contacts enables you to capitalize on relationships and credibility you've already built up with individuals in the past. If you've had any interaction with someone, he or she already has an impression of you (hopefully positive!) and knows what you're like to deal with. Since people prefer to work with a "known entity" rather than starting from scratch if they don't have to, you can capitalize on this. Moreover, as much as executives try, or say they try, to make vendor/resource decisions on the bare facts, a big part of the decision typically ends up being emotional. How do they feel? Do they like this person? With an already established relationship, you're starting out ahead of the game. And consulting relies heavily on

> *T*o be successful at trade shows, you need to use the same targeting strategy you use when selecting organizations to join and events to attend. Don't just give out business cards randomly. You don't want to contact or be contacted by people who can't use your services.

word-of-mouth, so leverage existing contacts to network with new ones.

Equally importantly, it gets you in the game to start with. It opens doors. You are many times more likely to get through the gatekeeper or get a return phone call (or even e-mail) if the contact knows you. Half the battle is getting in front of the right individual. By leveraging contacts, you only have to fight the other half of the battle: winning the project.

A few words on who is the 'right' individual. You not only need to get in front of the decision maker or key influencer to be successful, you also need to find someone who is ready, willing, and able. It's easiest to find people willing to meet with you. It's tougher to determine those actually able to make the hiring/contract decision. But it's true success when you find that individual who is also ready to pull the trigger: the time is right. It's a combination of the right need, the right ability, and the right timing.

Question: Should you develop a Web site and, if so, why?

Response: A Web site can be your on-line brochure. It's a fast, easy, inexpensive way to get a professional-looking presence for you or your company. As connected as everyone is today, it's very easy to direct people to your site to obtain information about you and your company. You can easily update it and add to it, so it can grow with you. In fact, many potential clients may try to look at the Internet first to see if you have a site. By setting up even a simple Web site, you are showing that you understand the way business works today, you are technically savvy, and you are a professional.

Question: Should you develop brochures and, if so, why?

Response: Printed brochures are another matter. They can be beautiful, but they are also expensive and fixed in content and look. If you are going to make this investment, you have to be very sure about what you are going to say and that those words will still be relevant months (and years?) out. Another angle is whether you are trying to position your consulting business as an individual practice or as a company. Typically, a brochure is not necessary if you are going to be an "independent consultant."

You are selling your ideas, experience, and personal capabilities. A well-developed biography and perhaps a few case studies will serve you well. If you are trying to develop a company that will include other consultants, a brochure may be more expected and will project a more serious and substantial image. One caveat: if you're a consultant who works in the design or image space (for example, graphic design), some printed pieces will be critical to show samples of your work, your style, and design solutions.

Most importantly, up front, make sure you have a professional-looking business card with matching letterhead, envelopes, and notepaper. Don't be tempted to get $10 cards that project the expertise of a $10/hour consultant.

A couple of creative ideas on this topic: With today's printing technology, you can do a surprising amount of 'desktop publishing' that enables you to put together professional-looking yet less-expensive materials. Just don't cut corners and end up with something cheesy; you'll just shoot yourself in the foot. Use strong, professional designs and high-quality paper. Another option is to develop a printed pocket folder. This way you can always vary and update the content by using individual sheets that get inserted into the folder. You're not locked into an expensive brochure, and you can customize the content to target it for a specific client.

Question: Does advertising help you find new clients?

Response: Generally not in broad-based media. It depends a lot on the industry focus and your specific experience. If you have considerable experience in one field or industry, you can target that segment using focused publications (typically either regional or national). If you have a tight-knit community, you can try local publications and test whether it works. Remember, it's a very network-intensive career.

Question: Is it worthwhile to write a column for your local newspaper?

Response: An excellent technique. This is a great way to get exposure, build up some name recognition, and gain credibility. Readers assume that a columnist is an expert in his or her field. They take it for fact that the writer knows what he or she is talking about ("or they wouldn't have hired him for the paper") and assume that there is an extensive screening process to find the best person. It's not always true, but readers don't know that. Many papers would be grateful for a knowledgeable resource to provide content to fill the pages, and you get to add a recognized credential.

Question: Is it worthwhile to participate in seminars?

Response: Conferences, seminars, expos, forums are all great ways to gain exposure. Since a primary goal is making contact with numerous people (the right people), this is a great way to accomplish it. You get excellent exposure to people in the right field or job function and gain great opportunities to network with them. Moreover, serving as a speaker or panelist endows you with additional credibility. It is assumed that you are an expert if you are chosen to speak. You then get to tout that you were featured at a specific event.

Question: Should I develop a joint marketing partnership with another consultant or company whose service or product is synergistic?

Response: Partnerships or, less formally, alliances can be a big help. They are a great way to expand your network and enhance the capabilities you can offer to a client. From a marketing standpoint, depending on your specifics, it can provide a way to stretch dollars and get an implied endorsement. However, be careful about maintaining your identity and anything that may be implied (but not intended) by the relationship.

Chapter Key Points

In order to build a successful consulting practice, you need to:

- Develop a sales plan.
- Take a sales training course.
- Develop a profile for the type of clients you want to have.
- Develop a list of organizations you want to join.
- It doesn't matter how good you are at what you do; if you can't get clients, all your expertise won't allow you to be a successful consultant. You need to be as diligent, well planned, and focused on getting clients as you are in providing your service.

HOW TO MAKE A SUCCESSFUL SALES CALL

LETTING THEM KNOW YOU CAN HELP SOLVE THEIR PROBLEMS

Before you take one step out of your office to go after new business, you need to develop a plan of action. You need to know what you are going to say and the best ways of communicating in order to increase your chances of success.

Developing a Sales Strategy

Just as you wrote out business, marketing, and sales plans, you need to have a plan for what you are going to say when you come to your first meeting with a prospective client. David Snyder, the author of How to Mind-Read Your Customers *(published by Amacom), is the chairman/CEO of Snyder, Inc. (www.mindread.net), and the former senior editor of* LEADERS *magazine, an international publication for world leaders in business, science, and the arts. He is a nationally respected expert on sales training and with a very successful sales training practice. He has a B.A. in English and Comparative Literature from the University of North Carolina at Chapel Hill, and holds an M.A. in psychology from Harvard University. Below is an interview with David Snyder about how to learn to sell and build sales momentum.*

Question: Should a consultant develop a sales plan?

Response: The trick for any consultant is to distinguish yourself from your competitors. That is why you need to develop a plan. Many consultants miss the simple things they can do, such as writing. Many are poor writers.

Question: What if you have never sold anything, but you are good at what you do? How can you learn to sell?

Response: It doesn't matter if you have ever sold anything. Whatever service you sell, you have to believe in it very strongly and passionately. People can tell if you are selling something just for the money. If they don't feel you are passionate about it, and if you don't know your product like the back of your hand, you won't make it as a consultant. Once you have the passion, you can then learn behavior tips that will enable you to sell yourself more effectively. You also need to keep in mind various things not to do, like calling people at the end of the day.

Question: What are the elements of good sales training programs?

Response: A good sales training program will teach you prospecting, how to interview clients, and the specific questions you should ask.

Question: What should be in that script?

Response: The first part of your script should give your company name. Don't choose a cute name. Make sure it can stand the test of time. Think about how your company name is going to sound and be perceived. You should also write out your company's mission. How will your company's mission improve your customer's business? Don't hire someone to write what you believe in. Spend time writing out what you believe in so people perceive your sincerity and buy your services. You don't want to come across as

> *S*hould an inexperienced salesperson develop a script of what he or she is going to say?
> "Yes and no! People should write down their sales pitch verbatim. You should also write down why a prospect would want to listen to you. You should get it down so well that it comes off naturally and seems to be the fabric of your being. One deadly mistake people make is coming into a sales meeting unprepared and trying to be spontaneous. Ninety-nine percent of the time it will backfire."

thoughtless and shallow. You need to write down your competitive strengths compared to others who offer the same services and be specific about what you have to offer customers.

Question: Should you practice your script on a friend or practice on the customer least likely to buy from you?

Response: Practice it on someone who is least likely to buy from you. You want to put yourself in the most demoralizing situation, one that is going to test you.

Question: When making your first contact with someone, should you send a letter or an e-mail?

Response: I am using e-mail more now and I send letters as attachments. If you can digitally put in your stationery, it looks more professional.

Question: What information should you bring to a first meeting and how should you follow up after a first meeting?

Response: Bring a physical copy of your letter in which you requested the meeting. Make sure that you pointed out everything you wanted to talk about in that letter. You want to create the meeting agenda, not someone else. Business isn't funny or a joke. Don't waste people's time. You should spell out the research you have done on the prospect's company and how you plan to help them. You should also try to mention someone else in the company or outside the company that the prospect knows. This lets the prospect know that you are smart, diligent, and care about your work.

Question: What are the most common mistakes people make in sales?

Response: The biggest mistake is that people come into a meeting trying to sell the client instead of coming across as a problem solver. The other common mistake people make is not being a good listener and telling the customer how you can help them.

Question: What is the best way to ask for the sale?

Response: There are so many courses on how to close a sale. You don't ask them for the sale if they are interested. If you write the letter properly, if you get an introduction from someone, and you come into the meeting prepared to demonstrate the value you can bring them, you will get the sale. Show people you are a caring, diligent person.

I have met many talented professionals who went into consulting and failed because they didn't take the time to develop a sales plan and weren't willing to spend the money on proper training.

Prepare for Battle

Once you go through a training course, and before you go to your first meeting with a prospective client, make sure you do your homework. Nothing impresses a businessperson more than a consultant who has taken the time and initiative to procure the following information:

Prospect's Business Focus: Before you go to your first meeting, stop at the prospective client's office and pick up any marketing material they provide to their own prospective clients. Then review their Web site and print it out. I always bring a printout of a prospect's site with my notes in the margins. I bring out my notes during the meeting to show the prospect that I took the time to get to know his or her company.

Prospect's Competition: On the Internet, use a search engine, such as Yahoo (www.yahoo.com) or AltaVista (www.altavista.com), and enter the type of work your

Doing Your Homework

One of my clients introduced me to a company that provides promotional products for product launches in the health-care industry. Before I went to the meeting, I looked at the Web site to get a better understanding of what the company offered and spoke to people I knew who used promotional products to build brand awareness. When I went into the meeting, not only did I know the firm's business, but I had ideas that I thought would drive new sales for them. The combination of homework and ideas got me a contract.

prospect does and the state in which the company is located. The search engines will pull up the names of the companies that provide the same products and services in the same state as your prospect. If nothing turns up, then you can reenter the query and omit the state.

Prospective clients are impressed when you take the time to understand their competitors, and examining competitors will get your creative juices flowing. My taking the time to understand my prospect's competitors helped me obtain a contract. The client was Right Management (www.right.com), the world's largest outplacement firm. I met with their CIO, Howard Mark, to discuss rebuilding their Web site. I came to the meeting prepared, with a spreadsheet and a strengths-and-weaknesses analysis comparing Right Management's Web site with its two largest competitors'. Howard Mark was so impressed with the analysis I provided that he said no one else they had interviewed to work on the project had as detailed an understanding as I did and that he was going to recommend to the Executive Vice President of Marketing that they hire me.

Because of a confidentiality agreement I signed with Right after they became a client, I can't share the competitive analysis I did, but below is an example of another one I did for an insurance company.

Categories	Prospective Client	AIG Direct	Esurance	Amica
Company Information				
History	Y	N	Y	Y
Key Personnel	N	N	Y	N
FAQ	Y	Y	Y	Y
Testimonials	N	N	Y	Y
Affiliate/Partner Program	N	Y	N	N
Career Opportunities	N	N	Y	Y
Consumer Contact Information				
Telephone Numbers	Y	Y	Y	Y
E-mail Address	Y	Y	Y	N
Mailing Address	Y	N	Y	Y
Press Contact Information				
Name of Contact	N	N	Y	N
Contact E-mail	N	N	Y	N
Links to Press Releases	N	N	Y	Y
Educational Information				
Advice on Lowering Insurance	Y	Y	N	N
Advice on Auto Selection	N	N	N	N
Calculator (used and new cars)	N	Y	N	N
State Regulatory Insurance Contacts	N	N	N	N
On-Line Safety Certificate	N	N	N	N
On-Line Newsletter	N	Y	N	N
Discount/Special Programs				
Car Rental	N	N	N	N
On-Line Car Purchasing	N	N	N	N
On-Line Parts Purchasing	N	N	N	N
Antique Car Sales	N	N	N	N
Car Clubs				
Type of Car	N	N	N	N
State	N	N	N	N
Show Calendars	N	N	N	N

FIGURE 9-1. Competitive analysis for insurance company (continued on next page)

Categories	Prospective Client	AIG Direct	Esurance	Amica
Content Languages				
Chinese	N	N	N	N
English	Y	Y	Y	Y
Japanese	N	N	N	N
Spanish	N	N	N	N
Technology				
Audio	N	N	N	N
LivePerson	N	N	N	N
Video	N	Y	N	Y
Application Process				
Driver	14	22	6	23
Vehicle	22	27	11	2
Household	2	5	3	4
Employment	1	1	1	1
Accident/Violations	1	2	1	1
Coverage	4	3	1	15
Total Questions	44	60	23	46
Asked for VIN	Y	Y	N	Y
Total Pages	6	14	3	7
Other				
Customer On-line Payments	N	N	Y	N

FIGURE 9-1. Competitive analysis (continued)

Amica.com

Strengths

- The Amica.com Web site is easy to understand.
- Information is presented in a straightforward manner.
- The Web site appears to be designed for insurance buyers who already know about automobile insurance and what they want to buy.
- The Web site offers other types of insurance.
- Home page has good graphics.

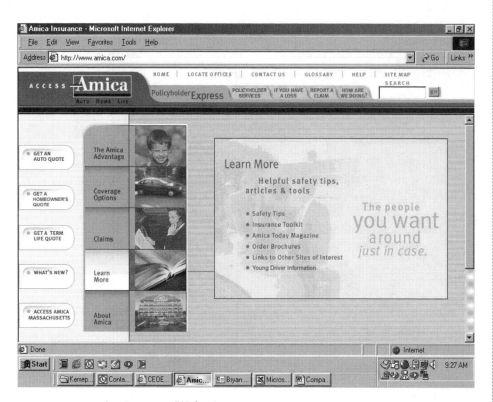

FIGURE 9-2. Amica.com Web site

- Home page allows users to access information about to the type of coverage they seek (auto, term, home, etc.) easily.
- It links users to other sites of interest.
- The on-line magazine offers useful up-to-date information of interest to users.
- [The magazine or the site] includes a special interest section aimed at young drivers.
- FAQ section covers many topics of interest to drivers.

Weaknesses
- The Amica.com Web site loads very slowly.
- Flash 5.0 is required to view some of the pages.
- The biggest drawback to using this Web site is that the user still has to speak to a company representative.

- The insurance claim form cannot be accessed without a policy number.
- Payments cannot be made on-line.
- Information on the different types of insurance coverage, limits, and deductibles is limited.
- Too many screens are required in trying to get a quote (e.g., if the VIN is not readily accessible, the user must go through three different screens to go to the next step in getting a quote).
- Instructions given are not always easy to understand, especially for novice users who might not be 100 percent comfortable with the Internet. (E.g., after the input of the information requested but before a quote is given, a screen pops up concerning "security issues." Unless one is very Internet savvy the screen only confuses the user.)
- Users must go to two different screens to input information about the make/model of the vehicle they want to insure.
- Contact numbers are not provided on the home page.
- No hours of service are provided.

Prospect's Customers' Perceptions

Finding out how customers perceive a prospective client isn't easy if the client provides services that are bought by a limited or hard-to-find market. If the prospective client is in the retail industry or you know people who use the prospect's products or services, contact them and ask them what they think.

Before I speak to prospects, I like to know what their clients say about them. I like to walk into the meeting showing prospects that I have some detailed understanding of their perceived strengths and weaknesses. I go to a prospect's

No. of Adults	Gender	Age	No. of Children	Age	No. of Vehicles	Amt of Time	Day of Week	Time	Data-Time
1	M	24	0	0	1	5	Wed	7 am	1
1	F	30	0	0	1	5	Wed	2 pm	1
2	M/F	35	0	0	2	7	Wed	7 pm	1
2	M/F	60	0	0	2	7	Thurs	7 am	1
2	M/F	40	2	16/18	3	10	Thurs	7:30 pm	1
1	M	40	2	16/18	2	10	Fri	9 am	1
1	F	45	2	16/18	2	10	Fri	5 pm	1
1	M	18	0	0	1	5	Sun	7 am	1
1	F	18	0	0	1	5	Sun	1 pm	1
1	F	50	0	0	1	5	Sun	7 pm	1
Questions	Number								
Driver	23								
Vehicle	2								
Household	4								
Employment	1								
Accid't/Violat.	1								
Coverage	15								
Total Quest.	46								
Asked for VIN	Yes								
Total Pages	7								

FIGURE 9-3. Web site visitors

Web site or look through their marketing materials to see whom they list as past clients. I call the clients and tell them I am thinking of using XYZ Company and would like to talk to someone who used them to get unbiased references. Below are two samples of what I do to prepare.

Example One

Below are five interviews I conducted about an information services company (that I eventually got as a client) and the results. I learned why clients chose the company, what they liked about them, areas my prospect could improve on, whether they would recommend the company, and new products and services the company could offer.

Question: Why did you choose Kadoch Solutions?

Respondent 1: We chose them because our president was friends with the owner of Kadoch Solutions and we are going to partner with them on some projects.

Respondent 2: They solicited a proposal on an infrastructure product, we liked the proposal, which was very thorough, and their price was competitive.

Respondent 3: A couple of years back, we had hired another company to develop software, and that company recommended Kadoch. That company didn't do such a good job and Kadoch now handles our infrastructure and software development.

Respondent 4: It was recommended by Ernie Jones, the attorney for Kadoch Solutions.

Respondent 5: We had no real IT support here because we aren't big enough. We hired them because we needed that type of support and we needed a group that could handle a variety of tasks, both hardware and software.

Question: What do you like most about working with Kadoch Solutions?

Respondent 1: They are very knowledgeable about what they are doing, very conscientious, and meticulous about noting everything they do and the process they use to accomplish it. Their people are very nice and easy to get along with, and they are usually here on time. If they can't be here on time or can't complete a task, they always let us know they are going to be late and when they plan to finish a task. You are never left wondering about anything.

Respondent 2: The quality of the individuals and their responsiveness has been terrific. We have been able to outsource expertise to Kadoch, and we didn't want to have to purchase that support internally, but we needed it when we needed it. We couldn't afford to get the quality of people Kadoch has recruited either. Scott Kushner is a class act and has been very good for us.

Respondent 3: They provide a level of organization that helps to keep us focused on various projects. The original vendor who wrote our software did not do a good job and Kadoch did a good job of fixing and improving it. The people are excellent to deal with personally and professionally. They are very good at responding to problems and solving them.

Respondent 4: The people are capable, responsive, and knowledgeable.

Respondent 5: I like the flexibility and knowing they are there when we need them. Even if we didn't sign up for a particular service, it's nice to know they can accommodate us. I like their business model because of the flexibility. They fill in the holes where you need it. Where we were weak, Kadoch was able to fill in those areas.

Question: Would you recommend them to other companies?

Response: Four said "yes" and one said "no."

Question: Who else did you consider before you hired Kadoch Solutions?

Respondent 1: We had used small, independent consultants, but they weren't as knowledgeable, and, if they were sick or backed up, they didn't have anybody to send to us to support our systems. You can't have your systems going down and not know when someone can come out to support them. That can kill your business.

Respondent 2: It was based on the U.S. Interactive recommendation.

Respondent 3: My son was a network guy and did it sometimes, but he moved on. We didn't speak to any other firms once we met Kadoch.

Respondent 4: We had used a lot of other firms before them for a variety of projects, but they couldn't cover the wide variety of platforms that Kadoch could, and the other firms typically overcharged us for services, which never happens with Kadoch. We had worked with Microage, IDSI (Philadelphia), Mtec, and JVC Technology.

Question: Where do they fall short?

Respondent 1: We are doing light IT stuff. I can't see any areas of improvement. Speaking from our company's perspective, they have everything we need. Maybe they could supply programmers to help on projects.

Respondent 2: Project-oriented software development. This isn't an expertise that they have, but it would be great if they offered it.

Respondent 3: The only problem we had was how they handled the management of our account. They needed to communicate better the changes they were making, but we haven't had that problem since and they did a good job of transitioning.

Respondent 4: David is working on a forward budget plan for us. He needs to tie it in to our company as it grows. He needs to understand what we can afford and develop plans that scale up to what we can afford.

Respondent 5: They need to be better at completing tasks. There seem to be some loose ends that don't always get cleaned up.

Question: What is your biggest day-to-day IT concern?

Respondent 1: Maintaining data integrity on our various projects, followed by desktop support.

Respondent 2: I don't have any because we are being phased out.

Respondent 3: There are two things. With our original system, we have had a lot of performance issues and we have lost employees because of it. The second concern is developing our new product and making sure it is easy for our clients to use. We would like our products delivered faster, but we have learned the hard way that, in order to make sure there are no problems with our products, the work needs to be done methodically. A big strength of Kadoch is that they help manage that anxiety and show us the value of being patient.

Respondent 4: That the equipment keeps running and to make sure we don't lose our data because of a catastrophe.

Respondent 5: Keeping our networks up and running until we are sold.

Example Two

One of my clients provides marketing support to chemical companies. Before I met with my then-prospective client, I contacted four business associates who were marketing professionals in the chemical field and asked them what they thought of the prospect's work. I showed the client the following results.

Client Perceptions of Smith Marketing
Strengths

- Strong understanding of the pharmaceutical and medical device market
- Strong understanding of marketing to physicians

- Excellent ability to deliver quality work on schedule
- Fair price for work

Areas of Improvement
- Need to educate clients on Smith's full range of capabilities
- Need to step back after a recommendation and allow the client to make the final decision
- Need to improve quality of copywriting
- Need to be more of a full-service agency

Opportunities
- Distance learning
- Public relations
- Showing clients how new technologies, such as mobile phones, can be used to deliver marketing messages successfully and increase sales

Suggestions for Improvement
- Cross-train account and project managers concerning ferreting out new opportunities and educating clients about new Smith Group services
- Develop white papers showing how Smith Group was able to solve a problem or run a successful campaign and the outcome of the solution and/or campaign
- Develop seminars focused on using various technologies to increase visibility and sales

> *I have found that many employers become so embroiled in the day-to-day running of the business that they have become disconnected from customers and their employees, so their views about what is best are, in many cases, no longer relevant. Don't take the leader's word regarding problems or needs the company has. Talk to the rank-and-file employees who are on the ground dealing with problems and opportunities.*

Employees' Perceptions of Client's Products/Services

Before I go into a meeting with a prospective client, I try to talk to employees to gauge how they feel about the company's product/service and how it can be improved. I try to get substantive information about how the employees view the strengths and weaknesses of the company.

Below is a sample interview I conducted before a meeting with a prospective client and the types of information I received from employees.

Question: What is the company's mission?

Response: RKB provides cost-effective proactive network administration. We try to tie them in to a team of cost-effective resources.

Question: What is RKB's competitive advantage?

Responent 1: Our competitive advantage is our business model and motivation: How we provide programs like this cost-effectively.

Responent 2: Our ratio of sales versus technical staff. There are usually one or two salespeople to three engineers. Our ratio is 2 to 25. We are focused on sales support.

Responent 3: We focused on acquiring only a few new customers a month.

Responent 4: We are the opposite of the retainer world. Our peers take that money and don't provide anything until there is a need. We provide services and the customer is billed on a monthly program. Our competitors have a use-it-or-lose-it mentality with their retainers.

Question: What is the process you use for selling a client? (step-by-step)

Response:
- The internal person makes cold calls.
- Qualifying the cold calls. I will ask them the number of computer users and their computer environment and whether they use outside vendors.
- I then make a visit and I will go over our whole pitch. We focus on delivering the RKB Connection. We are looking for a long-term customer.
- I then give them our one-page contract to review.

Question: What is the difference between competitors' retainers and your monthly charge to a client?

Response: The difference is that, with a retainer, once you have paid the retainer the company draws down on the amount of money. The difference is that we have the same person who comes in every month and doesn't have to be brought up to speed. Just as importantly, we are being proactive and we head off problems before they happen.

Question: How do you get your sales leads?

Response: We get 75 percent from cold calls, 20 percent from customer base and referrals, and 5 percent from the phone book.

Question: Why have you stayed at RKB so long?

Response: I like the people. I am treated fairly. I am fairly compensated. I believe in the product. If Sydney left I would probably follow him. Sydney cares about the employees and seems to always want to do the right thing.

Question: Why has RKB kept you for so long?

Response: I have a good work ethic. I try to help in any area they want me to. I always apply effort and I enjoy my job with a passion.

Developing Original Ideas

After you have spoken to clients and researched competitors, write down a couple of ideas based on what you have learned. I am sure you are thinking that the prospective client will take your ideas and implement them without you or that the client will give the ideas to another contractor who may be less expensive. That is a chance you need to take in the beginning, until you have developed a base of clients.

I have never had a prospective client take one of my ideas and do it themselves. Most prospective clients are impressed that you have given some thought to their problems and have some ideas, and are relieved that you will take ownership of your ideas and implement them on your own or run with them.

Client Presentation

After I have done my homework, I put together a brief analysis of what the prospect has done, what the competition is doing, and some of my own thinking on what the client needs to do to improve their competitive position. Below is an example of a presentation I gave a client whose Web site needed redevelopment. The CIO and director of marketing were so impressed with my knowledge that I got two contracts from them.

Kramer Communications Analysis and Recommendations

Overview

Feldman Management Consultants has five target audiences it serves:

- **President/CEO:** Presidents of companies are looking for human resource partners who will help them make acquisitions and downsizing smoother in order not to disrupt the company and not lose valued employees. Presidents are also looking for organizations that can help develop future leaders in the organization.
- **Human Resource Managers:** Human resource managers are interested in providing smooth transitions for outplaced employees and leadership training for managers, especially in the information-systems department. The IT department is the most difficult department for which to attract and retain talent. HR managers are also looking for quality employees to fill positions, and would prefer not to have to retain an executive search firm to find talent.
- **Chief Financial Officer:** Chief financial officers are looking to keep outplacement transition and executive-recruiting costs down.

- **Outplaced Professionals:** Outplaced professionals are going through the most difficult period of their professional lives. They feel that they were set adrift and don't add value in the corporate community. They are looking for guidance, answers, and opportunities to get back into the corporate game and feel successful again.
- **Investors:** Investors are made up of individuals, institutional money managers, financial planners, and plan sponsors. They are interested in understanding management's vision of the future and its plans for growing the company.

When you develop a Web site, you should focus on four areas:
- Mission—What is the company trying to accomplish with the Web site?
- Functionality—The user-friendliness of the site.
- User Reward—Giving targeted users reasons to bookmark the site so they will return.
- Owner Benefits—Capturing valuable information that can be used in prospecting, marketing, and improving client services.

Mission
The mission of the Feldman Management site is to show all five target audiences that Feldman Management is visionary, practical, and provides a high level of service that will help them to become successful in the future.

Functionality
Because the site is being used by busy corporate people and outplaced professionals who don't have a high-speed connection, the graphics have to download quickly and the site must be easy to navigate. Within the next year, Feldman will have to think about providing distance learning through its Web site, which dovetails with its concept of remote access. It's a big expense that the company isn't ready for at this time.

User Reward
Users need compelling reasons to bookmark the site. Below is a chart of elements that would encourage users to bookmark it. Those elements are shown in the chart on the top of the next page, by user. You will see a comparison in the competition section.

Owner Benefit
Feldman Management gathers contacts and user information in the following ways:
- requests for brochures, investor and media kits
- access to the matching programs

President/CFO	HR Managers	Investors	Outplaced Professionals
Executive Briefings	White Papers	Stock Quote	CEO Insights
CEO Insights	HR Views	Analyst Comments	HR Views
Feldman CEO Interview	Job Bank	Financial Information	Job Bank
	Feldman Matching Svsc.	CEO Interview	Resume Posting
	Seminars	Press Releases	HR Site Links
	Research Studies	Annual Meeting Dates	Book Reviews
	Published Articles		Entrepreneurial Interviews

- on-line resumes
- applications to work at Feldman Management
- registration for events

Old Site Map

The old site map had an overwhelming number of buttons, which could be confusing to the user and made it difficult to develop a good creative treatment. My suggestions for new buttons compared to the old buttons are shown below.

New Menu Buttons	Old Menu Buttons
Corporate Information	About Feldman
New Investor Information	Investor Relations
Right Events	Feldman News
Client Services	Feldman Events
Career-Transition Services	On-Line Client Service Center
Consulting Services	What's New
Site Map/Search	Don't Miss
	Free Subscription
	Send Info/Contact
	Career-Transition Services
	Consulting Services
	Site Map

Site Recommendations

- Feldman Management Consultants' corporate colors should be used on the site so the marketing message is consistent. The menu bar could have two colors. This would make the user aware that there are two separate types of information. For example:

Blue

- Corporate Information
- News/Investor Information
- Feldman Events
- Client Services

Red

- Career Transition Services
- Consulting Services
- Site Map

Suggestions for design elements of a Web site include the following:

- Feldman Management's 800 number should be at the bottom of each page. Having to search everywhere for telephone numbers is very frustrating to users. (Note: Look at the Tastykake Web site. You have to go on a treasure hunt on this business-to-consumer site to find out how to contact that the company.)

- We can use links like E-Trade, Disney, VeriSign, and other sites do to drive users to important parts of the site such as new information, subscriptions to newsletters, and so on.

- For users to obtain access to white papers, research, and other materials, we should have them fill out a subscription and then automatically e-mail them when changes to the site occur. This will also inform us who is accessing the site so we can send them invitations, follow-up information, and so forth.

- Executive profiles should have pictures and their e-mail addresses. The Intuit Web site (www.intuit.com) is a good example of this idea.

Competitive Comparison

I looked at the information that Feldman Management has on the site to attract repeat users and compared it to what the competitors are doing, as shown in the chart at the top of the next page.

	Feldman	Lee Hecht Harrison	Manchester USA	Drake Beam
Executive Briefings	Yes	Yes	Yes	No
CEO Insights	No	No	No	No
CEO Interview	No	No	No	No
White Papers	Yes	Yes	No	Yes
HR Views (for HR prof.)	No	No	No	No
Job Bank	Yes	Yes	Yes	Yes
Matching SVCs.	Yes	Yes	Yes	Yes
Seminars	Yes	Yes	Yes	Yes
Research Studies	Yes	Yes	Yes	Yes
Published Articles	Yes	Yes	No	Yes
Stock Quote	No	No	No	No
Analyst Comments	No	No	No	No
Financial Information [This is listed in line 3.]	No	No	No	No
Press Releases	No	No	No	No
Annual Meeting Dates [This is listed in line 2.]	No	No	No	No
HR Views (for Job Seekers)	No	No	No	Yes
Résumé Posting	Yes	Yes	Yes	Yes
HR Site Links	Yes	Yes	Yes	Yes
Book Reviews	No	No	No	Yes
Entrepreneurial Interviews	No	No	Yes	No

Ten Questions to Ask at the First Meeting

You have done your homework, but before you walk into the meeting make a list of questions you would like to have answered. Here is the list of questions I typically ask prospective clients and the order in which I ask them.

1. Why did you agree (or ask) to meet with me? I ask this question because it helps me frame my presentation. Asking this question gets the prospective customer on my side, psychologically. The prospect usually responds by saying, "I asked to meet with you because our salespeople tell me that few prospective clients know who we are and we need help with our marketing," or "We are launching a new service and we need someone to develop a plan."

2. How can I help you? Some of the information I'm seeking can be found in the response to the first question. I use this question to dig deeper. For example, I might ask the prospect if they want my help in developing a plan, implementing a plan, or both, and how soon they want the project completed.

3. Have you tried to tackle this problem before? If so, what were the results? It is important to know whether the prospect has attempted to do what they ask you to do. If they tried what they are asking you to do, you want to know why their efforts failed. You need to know what was done, how much money and time were spent, and what the client's expectations were. Once you know this, you will know whether the client's expectations were realistic and if your ideas are better than what was attempted.

4. Who is in charge internally for solving this problem? Find out who was in charge of the project that failed and whether the individual still works for the company. You want to know this because, if the person is still working at the company, he or she may be able to provide valuable information about why the project failed. You then want to know who represents the client internally, what his or her background is, and whether he or she will understand what you do and give you the support you need to succeed.

Before you agree to take on the contract, make a mental note to meet with the internal representative to determine whether you can work with that person. More than likely he or she will be at the initial or a second meeting.

5. Is the company's mission the same as what is stated on your Web site? Most mission statements are superficial. Therefore, you have to find out what the company is truly trying to accomplish at your meeting with the company leadership or the individual who wants to retain you. It doesn't matter whether the project is external or internal.

Understanding the company's mission will give you insight into company's financial focus and business ambitions. Knowing what the company's mission is enables me to understand what they are trying to accomplish. Once I know that, I can provide the most appropriate advice. Surprisingly, many company mission statements are not worth the paper or the cyberspace they occupy.

6. What is the profile of your ideal customer? If my prospect is targeting a specific kind of customer, I want to know the industry, financial size, number of employees, and who in the company would be contacted. I hope, through my research, that I have already answered this question, but I need the prospect to confirm my conclusions.

7. Who do you view as your competitors? The prospect will either confirm my understanding of the competition or tell me whom they view as the competition now and in the future. Knowing the competition will drive a lot of my decisions on the course of action I should take.

8. How do you currently market and sell your product/ service? Asking this question helps me determine what I should recommend and provides me with ideas concerning the tactics and strategies I should consider. Companies hire consultants to increase revenues, reduce costs, or improve efficiencies, which affects both revenue and costs. If you understand how a company sells its product or service, you will know how to apply your knowledge in order to provide the best service.

9. What strategies and tactics have been most successful for you? I want to know the answer to this question so I don't waste time suggesting the same solutions. Also, I want to think about how I can improve on what they view as success. I once had a client who viewed client seminars as the best way of attracting new clients. I told the client that I liked and appreciated their success with client seminars, but I thought they could reduce their costs and increase their closure rate by partnering with companies that would leverage their contacts for them. My client liked the idea and retained me to find suitable partners.

10. When do you want this problem solved and how much have you budgeted? Never be afraid to ask the most crucial question. Countless times I have met with prospective clients who didn't have either a budget or a time line for solving a problem. Many times prospects won't give you a budget because they are afraid that if they tell and you can do it for less, they will have wasted money. You need to ask this question so you have an idea of how serious and how soon a prospect will retain you. The majority of companies typically take 90 to 120 days to consummate a deal unless it is an emergency or the client has been searching for a solution for a period of time.

After I have the answers to these questions, I can develop a proposal based on what I have learned.

Chapter Key Points

All of the planning in the world won't do you any good if you don't execute your sales plan. You need to do the following to close sales:

- Take a sales training course.
- Conduct research to best understand your prospect's needs and how you can provide the greatest value.

> 🔑 Make a list of questions before you meet your prospective client and don't just shoot straight from the hip.
>
> 🔑 Finally, don't be afraid to ask for the sale. Unless you are independently wealthy, you can't afford not to ask prospects for the sale.

CHAPTER 10

DEVELOPING, BILLING, AND COLLECTING FEES

GETTING FULL PAY FOR VALUE ADDED ◀

The questions that baffle most consultants when they are starting are what to charge clients for their services, when to bill the client, and how to collect the fees. At the beginning, every consultant wrestles with the following questions:

1. Do I charge clients by the hour?
2. Do I charge a fixed price for projects?
3. Do I charge by the project?
4. Do I ask for my fee in phases (half up front, a quarter on delivery of half the project, and the remaining amount when the project is completed)?
5. Do I complete the project first and then bill the client?
6. Do I accept stock or stock options for all or part of my fee when dealing with startup or small companies?
7. Should I charge a client a low fee initially to get the job so I can prove my worth?
8. Should I charge a low fee and build in bonuses for myself based on the success of the project?
9. Should I charge a combination project fee and percentage of the revenue or savings my clients realize as a result of my work?
10. Should I be compensated for introductions that lead to new sales or savings for clients?

During the course of writing this book and interviewing a variety of very successful consultants, I found that there were many ways to develop fee structures and no one way was the right way. There are two issues you have to keep in mind as you try to figure out your answers to the questions above.

Financial Requirements

What do I need to charge and how much revenue do I need to bill for to pay all of my expenses?

Because you are selling time, you need to think in terms of the number of hours you need to bill to pay all of your expenses. Remember, you have to pay the following expenses:

- business supplies
- computers and software
- health care
- Internet access
- federal, state, and local business and personal taxes
- membership dues
- travel expenses

You need to keep in mind that you probably can't work more than 70 hours in a week or you will burn out. More than likely you will work between 50 and 60 hours in a week.

You have to consider your personal expenses and how much income you need to generate in order to pay your personal bills and build up a reserve because there will be slow times when income either is not coming in or is reduced. If you don't factor in these issues, you will find it difficult to survive.

*B*etween a quarter and a third of your time will be spent on marketing and selling your services and a third to a half your time will be spent on doing client work. The rest of your available time will be spent doing administrative chores.

Competition

What is the competition charging or what are clients willing to pay for what you do?

It has been my experience that clients rarely ever like to pay by the hour and/or not have a cap on the number of hours. 99 percent of clients I have dealt with prefer fixed-price contracts and, if the contract needs to be adjusted because of changes in the agreement, most are willing to either pay more for the new deliverables or adjust and reduce already agreed-on deliverables.

You have to find out what the competition charges for a similar project and what a client feels is a fair price. To get a handle on this, you have to understand how your clients make money, how much they make, and their profit margins. If you work with retailers, you know they work on thin margins and they are very price-sensitive. On the flip side, money managers have high margins, their businesses are scalable, and money isn't usually an issue.

Fee Development Questions

Now that you know what the two key issues are for developing your fee structure, you can begin to tackle the 10 questions concerning fee development:

1. Do I charge the client by the hour?

Many businesses are used to dealing with lawyers and accountants who charge by the hour. Although this is the norm for these professions, most companies prefer to have a cap on the number of hours or on the overall project. Some clients who really understand a consultant's business will hear the flat-rate project price and ask the consultant to charge by the hour and cap the amount of hours. Once the number of hours is exceeded, the client can determine whether the consultant is efficient or inefficient, or that the client's expectations were unrealistic and the number of hours needs to be bumped up.

Pluses: An hourly rate is ideal if clients aren't precise about what they want to do or won't agree to the specifics in a proposal and want to be able to make changes on the fly. A friend of mine, for example, was an information technology consultant. The client knew what was wanted from a 50,000-foot level, but wasn't sure of the details. My friend told the client that, once they got started, he knew from experience that the client would want to make changes and that charging by the hour was the only way to keep the client focused and disciplined so that my friend could earn a fair wage.

Minuses: If you are an efficient consultant and you know clients are used to paying a certain fee for the type of service you offer, and that you can do that service in half the time, then charging hourly will prevent you from making a greater profit. An associate of mine develops marketing plans for pharmaceutical product launches and typically charges $50,000 per launch. The buyer had spent 10 years providing the same service as my associate and said he would prefer it if my friend charged by the hour and capped the number of hours. He knew the consultant was efficient and experienced, and knew the cost would fall somewhere between $30,000 and $40,000, even if my associate padded his hours. The client saved at least 30 percent off the fixed-price fee.

2. Do I charge a fixed price for the project?

Most clients prefer that consultants charge by the project so they know the cost of the project. Many companies have gotten stung when greedy, inept, or dishonest consultants have run up hours with nothing to show for it. One of my clients hired an IT consultant who ran up $30,000 in billings with little to show for it. After that my client refused to hire anyone, regardless of reputation, by the hour. Every project had to be billed as a fixed-price contract.

Pluses: I personally like a flat fee for a project. The client knows the fee is fixed and I know that I have to work fast and efficiently if I want the contract to be profitable. The client doesn't worry that I am taking advantage of them.

Minuses: There are many ways you can lose money on a fixed-price project. For example, you can underestimate the time it takes to complete. The client may not have told you everything or may want to add new elements to the project. This happens quite often.

If you are going to do a fixed-price contract make sure you get everything in writing.

3. Do I charge by the project, and if so, how much?
I like charging by the project because I know there is a beginning, a middle, and an end.

Pluses: I think it is best for the client because they get to see how you work and can decide if they want to continue to work with you. It also gives you a chance to see if you like working with the client.

Minuses: No downsides that I know of and everyone I have interviewed for this book feels that charging by the project in the beginning of a business relationship makes everything clean and orderly.

4. Do I ask for my payments in phases (half up front, a quarter on delivery of half the project, and the remaining amount when the project is completed)?
Many consultants charge a quarter to half their fee up front and receive the rest of their compensation as milestones are reached.

Twice, I have been burned by taking less than a third of my fee up front. One client told me they didn't have the money to pay me, and the other abandoned the project after I had put in a large number of hours. Both of these times, the people seemed honest and sincere, but, when it came time to honor their commitment, they left their integrity at the door.

Pluses: I am a big believer in charging up-front fees, and I typically ask as much as half and as little as a third up front. I have seen other consultants burned when they don't take part of their fee up front.

A colleague of mine, who follows the same philosophy that I do, took half of his fee in advance. The client said it wasn't acceptable, but he was in a hurry to get the project done and agreed to the fee structure. After my colleague produced what he thought was quality work, the client, much to my colleague's surprise, fired him, said he was incompetent, and asked my colleague for all or a prorated part of his fee back.

My colleague had never encountered this type of problem before and contacted a friend who knew this particular client. The friend said the client had fired three other consultants and that my colleague was lucky to have gotten half his fee up front. The friend guessed that the client was desperate because he ran out of consultants with my colleague's expertise. Fortunately, my friend had put in the contract that the retainer was nonrefundable and walked away financially unscathed.

Minuses: I don't think there is any downside to taking money up front. There will be the occasional client who may be insulted because they feel you don't trust them. I tell clients I do this because of my past experiences with clients refusing to pay, clients not being able to pay, or the client dying, which actually happened to a colleague of mine. The estate refused to pay my colleague's fee.

5. Do I complete the project first and then bill the client?
Gary Samartino, one of my colleagues I interviewed for this book, does only project work and always bills the client after the project is done. As you will see later in the book, Gary has been a very successful consultant for 15 years.

Pluses: You generate a lot of trust between you and the client. When you are finished, you can look forward to collecting a nice paycheck and, potentially, get more work from the client.

Minuses: As I mentioned before, well-meaning people can leave you holding the bag because they don't like the work you have done, they have run out of money, or their boss has killed the project along with the budget for it. I also don't want to be the bank for someone else's company. All too often, once a consultant finishes a project, the client is slow to pay. One of my clients, who does consulting work for large medical device companies, has had to go without pay for months at a time because of slow pay from clients. Never turn over the completed project until you are paid part or all of your compensation.

6. Do I accept stock or stock options for all or part of my fee when dealing with startup or small companies?

I have had a range of companies, especially startup and small companies, ask me if I would be willing to take stock options or barter services. If I like the management and the concept, I will accept stock options. To date, I have stock options in 16 companies and none have paid off.

Pluses: If you and the experts you have consulted believe that your client has the potential to be a public company traded on one of the four major stock exchanges or might be bought by a larger company for a substantial price, then having stock options can be very lucrative.

Minuses: Another colleague of mine took 80 percent of his $100,000 fee in stock. He loved the product and felt his marketing skill would make a difference in the company's success. Unfortunately, the founder was a poor leader who didn't recognize his shortcomings and my friend lost his

Taking It in Stock

A colleague of mine did work for a major telecommunications company when it was in its infancy. The founders asked my colleague if he would take stock options in lieu of half his fee. My colleague agreed to take a third of his fee in stock options. A third of his cash fee would have been $15,000. Fortunately for my colleague, the company went public and he made $250,000. He was kicking himself for not taking more stock.

entire fee. Not only did he lose the cash he could have earned, but the Internal Revenue Service does not allow you to write off the tax losses incurred when you trade fees for stock options.

I won't and would not encourage anyone to take an entire fee in options. That is taking too great a risk and you won't be able to support yourself.

7. Should I charge a client a low fee initially to get the job so I can prove my worth?

Practically all consultants start out by offering their service for a below-market fee in order to break in and get their first client. The only consultants that I have ever met who haven't had to do that are well-known business leaders and individuals who were retained by their former employers.

Pluses: If your skills and knowledge are as good as or better than others who offer the same service, then whether you get the project or not will probably come down to price. Having a lower price is a great incentive for someone to hire you.

Minuses: You don't want prospective clients to think you will always offer below-market prices. The biggest downside is that prospective clients will think the reason you charge less than your competitors is because you aren't as good or don't have the experience. Many times buyers are willing to pay market prices for first-time consultants. Remember that you have a body of work that has led you to the point of starting your own consulting practice.

8. Should I charge a low fee and build in bonuses for myself based on the success of the project?
Many consultants, especially in the field of sales, are willing to take bonuses based on results because they are used to that.

Pluses: Clients love to tie performance to fees. If the performance is good or great they don't mind paying the consultant the bonuses because the buyer feels they were earned. I do this a lot, even after being a consultant for over a decade. I charge a low fee so that I have some money coming in and the buyer has had to take some financial risk. My bonuses are usually set at double or triple what I would have earned on an hourly basis.

Minuses: You don't have control over whether your marketing, sales, or any work that you do will yield results. Therefore, you are taking a tremendous financial risk. When I first started, I agreed to take my entire contract in a performance bonus. This was a huge mistake, because the client wouldn't give me the attention he would have if he

Creative Billing

One of my clients is a money-management firm. The service I provided was helping the client obtain speaking engagements. I offered to perform this task using a combination fee structure that included a small monthly retainer and $10 per person who attended his speaking engagements. This arrangement convinced the client that I had confidence in my ability to deliver results and forced the person to make a cash commitment to me. The end result was that I made three times as much money as if I had charged for the service.

were paying some of my fee in cash. When results were slow to materialize, he retained someone else and paid them both cash and a bonus. The person he hired didn't produce anything, but at least that person got paid. If you are willing to work for free, then the person hiring you will not value your work.

9. Should I charge a combination project fee and percentage of the revenue or savings my clients realize as a result of my work?

The difference between a low fee/bonus method of payment and the project fee/percentage of revenue or savings is that you can earn more by taking a percentage and the fees will be paid to you longer.

Pluses: You are getting the best of both worlds. You are receiving a project fee, so you are receiving some income up front and the client has a vested financial interest. I have taken a percentage of the revenue on several projects and it has worked out well. Taking a percentage of the revenue or savings makes a consultant feel like a partner in the venture.

Minuses: The only downside is that you may be taking less cash up front and, therefore, risking time, which is the same as money, for your efforts.

10. Should I be compensated for introductions that lead to new sales or savings for clients?

Why shouldn't you make money off of introductions that you provide for clients? You have worked hard and invested a lot of time and money in developing business contacts.

Pluses: A great part of my appeal for my clients is my network of contacts. When I ran a trade association, my contacts made members millions of dollars; the only thing we received was their membership fee. When I left the trade association, people still wanted to trade off my contacts.

Minuses: Some clients are put off by consultants who ask for a fee for an introduction that leads to a sale. They feel that they pay you for services, and this should be part of the service you provide. There is no hard-and-fast rule concerning whether you should or shouldn't charge for introductions. No matter what a client is paying me in cash, I always ask if I can get a percentage of a deal that came through one of my contacts. The worst thing a client can say is "no." If you handle it, delicately you shouldn't offend your client and you may make what my father calls "found money."

I interviewed Phil Webster, who has 35 years of investor relations and corporate communications experience as a consultant and as the principal public affairs officer for three New York Stock Exchange-listed companies. Prior to opening his consulting practice, he served as the Vice President of Public Affairs for Scott Paper Company with responsibility for the company's worldwide communications. At Brunswick Corporation, Phil had responsibility for corporate and financial communications. As the Vice President of Damon Corporation, Phil led the company's worldwide corporate communications, investor relations, and government relations efforts. He has a B.A. from Boston University in communications. Phil provides insights on how he got into consulting and how he figured out what to charge.

Question: Why did you become a consultant?

Response: Being a consultant and an independent entrepreneur was something I always wanted to do after I had gained a sufficient amount of corporate experience to be of value to my clients.

Question: How much money did it take to start your consulting practice?

> *My standard response to a request for an introduction, which makes my wife laugh, is "how can I financially participate through my introduction?" Some people who were so used to getting my contacts for free were shocked initially. After they thought about it, they were agreeable to paying me five to 20 percent, depending on the margins of the potential transaction. Over the last couple of years I have made $50,000 just by picking up the telephone or sending an e-mail.*

Response: It took $50,000 in seed capital.

Question: Did you write a business plan for yourself?

Response: I wrote a detailed business plan before I formed The Webster Group in 1988. I interviewed a number of people who could be potential clients and asked them what services they needed from a consultant, where the voids were in the services currently available to them, and the characteristics they valued in the firm or individuals providing those services. I then structured my business plan and the firm around client needs, and have followed that plan since I began the firm, changing it to fit changing circumstances.

Question: How did you figure what to charge your clients?

Response: I asked a great number of my colleagues who were consultants what their charges were. Then I looked at what the market would bear and what my costs were, and attached a reasonable margin. Over time, I learned what clients would pay for the number of hours and value-added we brought to the assignment.

Question: Do you ask for a retainer before you do your work and, if so, how much?

Response: We don't ask for a retainer up front. Occasionally, when we do projects we might ask for a third up front if the fee is already known. For ongoing projects or continuing work, we do not. I think it is insulting to the client to be asked to pay us before we do the work. If you are working for someone who, because of their financial condition, you aren't sure will pay you, then you might ask for part of the payment up front.

Question: How long did it take you until you were making the same salary and benefits you had when you were employed by someone else?

Response: It took nine months to break even and a year and a half to earn what I was making on the corporate side.

Question: How did you get your first client?

Response: My first client was my former employer, Scott Paper Company. The better question is: How did I get my second client, which was PolyGram, the leading music recording company? The treasurer was a close friend and he hired us to help them with investor relations. The company was located in Britain and that opened the door for new clients on the Continent, as well as other industry-leading clients such as Nokia, GlaxoWellcome, and Credit Suisse, among others.

Question: Have you ever had a client who refused to pay and, if so, what did you do?

Response: We had a client unable to pay us because of bankruptcy. I can't think of a client who has refused to pay us. We have had a few clients, when we had negotiated the fee in advance, dispute the amount of our bill. For the sake of good client relations, we adjusted our bill.

Question: If you have one piece of advice you'd give to someone starting a consulting business, what would it be?

Response: Make sure you have the experience and inner fortitude to deal with good times as well as bad. Make sure you have the internal qualities and drive to follow through with your business plan and be successful. You should diversify your service offerings within reason. There are periods of time when your one service will be out of favor and you will need to be able to offer other services. Services will also change over time. In our first nine years, clients would ask us if we knew someone they could hire to do what we recommended. That is how we got into executive recruiting. Consulting is a fluid thing and an ever-changing discipline, and one needs to change with the times.

Show and Tell

The spreadsheet I developed (below) shows prospective clients what they would pay for my services for a year and how hiring me is a less expensive alternative to hiring a full-time employee. I use Salary.com (www.salary.com) to show the cost of hiring a manager with some experience and the lowest-level person who has virtually no experience. I tell the client that I haven't included the cost of running the advertisement to attract the candidate, training, unemployment insurance, and severance pay. Once clients see this spreadsheet, they usually retain me.

Manager (from Salary.com)		
Categories	Internal Employee	Kramer
Salary	$61,000	$42,000
Benefits (25%)	$15,250	0
Office Space	$5,250	0
Telephone	$1,200	0
Office Supplies	$600	0
Computer Equipment/ Software	$2,000	0
Conferences/Seminars	$1,000	0
Total Cash Outlay	$86,300	$42,000

FIGURE 10-1. Internal vs. external (continued on next page)

Nonmanager, TwoYears Experience (Salary.com)		
Categories	Internal Employee	Kramer
Salary	$38,450	$42,000
Benefits (25%)	$9,613	0
Office Space	$5,250	0
Telephone	$1,200	0
Office Supplies	$600	0
Computer Equipment/ Software	$2,000	0
Conferences/Seminars	$1,000	0
Total Cash Outlay	$58,113	$42,000

FIGURE 10-1. Internal vs. external (continued)

Chapter Key Points

🔑 Developing your fee structure is one of the most important things you will do, because it tells prospective clients about the value you believe you bring and determines how much money you can make.

In order to develop your fees you need to do the following:

🔑 Develop a list of all business and personal expenses.

🔑 Figure out how many hours you are able and willing to work and subtract the number of hours you will spend marketing and selling your services.

🔑 Once you know how many hours you have left, what you will need to charge for those hours becomes clear.

🔑 Find out what your competitors charge.

DEVELOPING KILLER PROPOSALS

TELL THEM WHAT YOU'RE GOING TO DO FOR THEM ◀

*W*hen I first started my consulting practice, I wrote terrible proposals. Fortunately, I had a certain expertise that few people had. Also, my clients were much older than I was and willing to instruct me on what I needed to do to provide a quality proposal.

What was wrong with my proposals? They didn't convince clients that I understood the following things:

- *client's business*
- *purpose of the work they wanted me to do*
- *deliverables I would provide*
- *timetable for providing deliverables*
- *required client responsibilities and deliverables*

Stages of Proposal Submission

The biggest mistake first-time consultants make during the proposal phase of the interaction between themselves and a potential client is not realizing that making a proposal is a process. Most first-time consultants think they listen to the potential client, make notes, submit a proposal that the client signs, and then the relationship starts. Don't ever make the assumption that the first draft of your proposal will be accepted.

I can't tell you how many times clients have told me what they need and, when I give them a proposal, I have either misunderstood what they want, they have miscommunicated what they want, or they have decided they want something different. Many clients are also neophytes at hiring consultants and will wrongly assume that the proposal you are submitting is set in stone. When the prospect doesn't return your calls or hires someone else, you are left wondering what happened.

There are four steps to submitting a proposal.

Step One: While you are in the meeting with the client, take notes and repeat back to the client what you heard so you are clear on what the client perceives as the company's needs.

Step Two: Develop the proposal and mark it "Draft" in 24-point bold font on every page.

Step Three: Never e-mail a draft of the proposal to a client, even if they instruct you to. The only exception to this rule is if the client is out of the country and needs to move quickly. Set up a time to meet with the client to review the proposal. Remind the client from the beginning of the meeting that the proposal is a draft and that you want to make sure you understand their needs, who is responsible for what, the time line for getting things done, and the fees

> *Have someone review your proposal before you deliver it, to be sure you haven't put in the wrong client's name and that there are no grammatical mistakes. The first problem may sound unlikely, but it has happened to me because I reuse proposals and/or I inadvertently put in the wrong name.*

you think are appropriate. Write down the changes the prospect wants made to the proposal and verbally review the changes before leaving to redraft it.

Step Four: Redraft the proposal and highlight the changes you have made so the prospect can see them easily. Make an appointment with the client and review the changes. Once the client has approved the proposal, ask the client to sign the contract.

This process has served me well through 100 client engagements.

The Ten Most Important Elements of a Proposal

Some consultants submit proposals that require a tractor-trailer to deliver to a client. Other proposals are so thin you could wipe mustard off your face with them. I have written proposals for projects ranging from $5,000 to $100,000 and none of them required more than 10 pages of information. A proposal should include the following 10 elements:

1. Purpose: A one- or two-sentence description of what the client wants.

2. Objective: A few paragraphs describing what the client would like to accomplish with the project. I also describe what each group the client wants to reach with the project will get out of it once it is completed.

3. Description of Client: A description of what the client does and who they target for their product/service.

4. Process: This describes the process of how the project will be developed and completed.

5. Contractor Deliverables: Clients need to know what they are going to receive for their money.

> *O*nce a prospective client has invited you to make a proposal, the most important part of the proposal is your description of the process you will use to produce the result they are looking for. It also gives the buyer the chance to determine whether you really know what you are talking about. Take the time to really think through the process of how you plan to deliver the project successfully.

6. Client Responsibilities and Deliverables: Clients need to know what you expect from them.

7. Time Lines: Every client likes to know how long you will take to deliver your work. I have found that I make all of my deadlines; the problem is keeping the client on track to make their deadlines.

8. Financial Terms: The client wants to know what you expect to be paid and when you expect to be paid. I typically break my contracts up into three parts: a third to a half of the contract up front, a quarter on delivery of a set of milestones, and the rest after the client is satisfied with the final product.

9. Standard Policies: This tells the client what you will and won't bill them for outside of normal fees such as travel, materials needed to complete a project, telephone bills, and so forth.

10. Backgrounds of Service Providers: You should include one-page biographies of the individuals involved with the project. Clients like to know and be able to show their bosses or subordinates the backgrounds of the professionals in charge of the project so they can substantiate why the contractor was selected.

Below is a sample proposal. You will notice it covers all time items related to a good project proposal.

Deadlines and Penalties

One of the biggest mistakes I made in the past was not giving deadlines to clients for completing tasks and projects. I have had clients take as much as a year and a half to complete a small project. Now I put in a "penalty clause" for clients who don't complete their tasks by specific dates. If you don't do this, you won't collect your money and you won't have a completed project to show prospective clients.

Wahl Asset Management

For Internet Plan and Web-Site Development

The purpose of this proposal is to outline the consulting relationship that will lead to Web site development between Wahl Asset Management and Kramer Communications.

Objectives: Kramer Communications will work with the marketing department of Wahl Asset Management to develop a Web site that builds sales momentum with plan sponsors, pension consultants, and financial intermediaries and provides higher-quality service to current institutional and individual clients. This Web site will be set up to serve several different constituencies:

Plan Sponsors: Current and prospective public and private institutions with assets that need to be managed

Individual Investors: Current and prospective individuals who already have or are considering having their money managed by a small firm as opposed to a large retail money-management firm such as a Fidelity or Invesco

Pension Consultants: Provide information that will help the gatekeepers who represent pension plans in their selection of money managers.

Financial Intermediaries: Provide information to individuals who recommend money managers to individual and corporate clients seeking someone to oversee their defined benefits and contribution retirement plans.

Process and Deliverables

Phase One. Site Plan and Map Development

Kramer Communications will develop a Web site plan for Wahl Asset Management.

Phase One. Deliverables

Kramer Communications will begin the process by performing internal and external interviews.

Internal Research: Kramer Communications will interview the Chairman, executives in charge of marketing and customer service, and selected portfolio managers. The purpose of these interviews is to gain insight into the strengths of the firm and to ascertain how using the Internet to communicate with clients and prospective clients can mitigate any weaknesses the firm may have.

The types of questions we will ask are as follows:

- What makes Wahl Asset Management unique?
- What is the corporate culture?

- What types of clients are best suited for Wahl Asset Management?
- What are Wahl Asset Management's long-term asset goals?
- What types of information would Wahl Asset Management like to see on its Web site?

External Research: Kramer Communications will conduct qualitative research to gain an external perspective of the concept and to assess the competitive landscape as it relates to Web site usage. We will look at competitor Web sites, review industry trends, and conduct an initial review of existing information. Through this external research, Kramer Communications hopes to isolate the strengths of the concept that can be leveraged through the Internet and identify potential weaknesses the Internet may be able to help mitigate.

As part of this effort, we will interview three plan sponsors and three financial intermediaries. We will identify possible areas of competitive advantage and begin the process of developing a site strategy and plan. The types of questions we will ask are as follows:

- Why did you choose Wahl Asset Management to manage your institution or client's money?
- What impresses you about Wahl Asset Management?
- What types of information would you like to find on Wahl Asset Management's site?

Once the internal and external interviews are completed, Kramer Communications will write a plan to develop the site. The following outline describes the content of the plan:

- **Mission:** the purpose of the site and who the targeted users are
- **Content Description:** information that current and prospective plan sponsors, individual investors, pension consultants, and financial intermediaries would look for
- **Competition:** an analysis of sites of similar-size competitors to ensure that the Wahl Asset Management Web site is at least on a par with competitor sites and that, in future phases, the Wahl Asset Management site exceeds the competition
- **Marketing of Site:** best ways to market the site to create sales momentum
- **Product Sales:** how the products will be sold and delivered
- **Management of Site:** recommendation on whether a full-time, internal person needs to run the site initially or management of the site can be outsourced
- **Site Map:** describes the menu buttons and content that will be found on the site
- **Launch Plan:** provides a time line for developing the Web site
- **Technology Recommendation:** recommendation regarding which technology would be most cost-effective and scalable and best fit with Wahl Asset Management's current tech-

nology infrastructure, especially in regard to providing sponsors and individual investors access to their accounts

- **Developer Recommendation:** recommendation of the best regional Web-site developer to hire
- **Hosting Recommendation:** recommendation for which regional or national Web site-hosting service would provide the best service at the best price
- **Financial Forecast:** a financial forecast to get a handle on what the costs will be to build and maintain the site

Kramer Communications will review a draft of the plan with Wahl Asset Management executives. Once the plan is approved, development of the site will begin.

Phase Two: Design, Development, and Hosting of the Web Site

After Wahl Asset Management's executive committee approves the plan, a developer will be selected. Kramer Communications will act as Wahl Asset Management's advocate and work with the developer to coordinate creation of the Web site.

More specifically, this phase will include:

- formatting content as HTML and functional programming;
- page layout and design, including animation of selected elements;
- building multi-tested user access and system security control;
- development of real-time "interactive" tools;
- personalization and dynamic page generation.
- quality control infrastructure and testing;
- links to existing company databases, if required.

Once the development is completed and the URL (site name) is registered, Kramer Communications will interview several Web-hosting services and recommend one to host Wahl Asset Management's site.

Phase Three: Site Maintenance

Wahl Asset Management will determine whether it will make site changes and upgrades in-house or outsource those changes to a third party. If Wahl Asset Management decides to outsource future development, it will also have to decide whether it will have one of its employees interface with the Web-site developer or outsource this function as well to Kramer Communications.

Project Management

Marc Kramer will oversee development of the plan during Phases One and Two. After Phase Two, Wahl Asset Management will determine whether to outsource the rest of the management of the project to Kramer Communications.

Project Fees and Time Lines

This will be a high-priority assignment for Kramer Communications. The phases, time lines, and fees noted in the table below are initial estimates. If Wahl Asset Management at any time feels that it is necessary to modify or discontinue this agreement, Kramer Communications will implement this change within 30 days and Wahl Asset Management will be billed only for work completed through that time.

Phase One: The first phase of this project will begin within a week of Wahl Asset Management agreeing to the terms of the contract. The cost for Phase One will be $10,000.

Phase Two: Kramer Communications, as Wahl Asset Management's representative, will work with the Web-site developer to ensure that the work is of the highest quality and that the project is completed in a timely manner. The cost will be $150 per hour and won't exceed $5,000 per month, unless approved by Wahl Asset Management.

Phase Three: Wahl Asset Management will determine whether to retain Kramer Communications to work with in-house or outsourced developers for future changes on the site. The cost will be $150 per hour for Kramer Communications to interface with developers and won't exceed $2,500, unless approved by Wahl Asset Management.

Additional Costs and Professional Standards

Refer to attached description of Standard Professional Policies.

Acknowledgment and Acceptance

Please indicate your willingness to proceed with Phase One by returning one executed copy of this proposal and a deposit of $5,000 to Kramer Communications.

Acknowledged and Accepted

By: _____   _____

   Wahl Asset Management   Kramer Communications

_____   _____

   Date   Date

Standard Professional Policies

Additional Costs

Outside costs, such as for photography, illustration, typography, art materials, transcription services, and printing, incurred by Kramer Communications on behalf of a client, are billed with a standard industry mark-up. Pro-rata travel (coach airfare for domestic, business class for international flights) and related expenses, courier and delivery charges, facsimile and telephone charges are billed at cost. Applicable sales tax is charged in accordance with Pennsylvania Law.

Project Billing

Projects are billed on a monthly basis as work progresses. Billings include approved fees, outside costs, travel and related expenses, and applicable taxes. Payment is due 30 days from invoice date. Account balances over 30 days incur a late interest charge of 1.5 percent per month.

Project Budgets

Fee quotations for services offered by Kramer Communications remain in effect for 30 days from the date of the proposal and are subject to change thereafter. The client will submit any variations from the work outlined in the proposal in writing for approval before work is started.

Design Rights

Creative work developed by Kramer Communications and approved for use by a client becomes the exclusive property of that client after payment is received, consistent with industry standards.

Design Production

Final clearance and registration of creative work developed by Kramer Communications is the responsibility of the client and their legal counsel unless the obtaining of such rights is specifically requested during the course of a project. Designs, names, and trademarks created by Kramer Communications are not intended to infringe on the rights of others; however, due to the complexity of such rights, Kramer Communications cannot guarantee that its clients will be protected from the claims of others, no matter how inadvertent the cause.

Web-Site Development

An estimate for technical implementation will be submitted to the client for review and approval prior to the commencement of any work in developing a Web site. Payment for one-half of the technical development cost is required in advance of undertaking the site development work.

Confidentiality

Kramer Communications maintains strict sensitivity and confidentiality concerning all client information and material. Please initial below to show that you have read and understand this document.

_____

Client Initials

Marc Kramer's Biography

Marc Kramer is president of Kramer Communications, which provides Internet strategic marketing, sales and communications, business-plan development, and content-service strategy and project management. He is also a professional speaker and lectures on topics such as Internet marketing, sales networking, corporate entrepreneurship, and turning around distressed companies.

Marc is a former partner at USWeb, the world's largest Internet consulting firm, and prior to that was President of Mixed Media Works, an interactive company that produced Web sites for Rosenbluth International and CoreStates Bank, among others.

Before joining MMW, Marc started the Eastern Technology Council, the second-largest business technology council in the United States, with over 1,000 corporate members. He also launched and ran *Technology Times*, the second largest business technology newspaper in the United States; the Pennsylvania Technology Transfer Center; the Institute of Biotechnology and Advanced Molecular Medicine; the Penn State Technology Development Center; and the Pennsylvania Private Investors Group, the country's first formally organized investor angels' network.

Marc has also served as interim President/CEO of *Business Philadelphia* and *Seven Arts*, two large regional magazines.

Marc has received such awards as the *Inc.* Magazine Entrepreneur of the Year and American Electronics Association Spirit of America Award, and was named one of the Top Five Business Leaders under Age 40 in the Philadelphia region for three years in a row by the Philadelphia Jaycees.

This past fall, Marc's first book, published by the Tribune Company, *Power Networking,* hit the bookstores. This fall, his second book, *Executives' Guide to Managing Turnarounds*, published by Greenwood Publishing, will be released.

Marc has been quoted in over 40 publications including *The Wall Street Journal, Success,*

Fortune, Forbes, Inc., and the *Philadelphia Inquirer.* In 1993, Marc was featured on the cover of *Profit,* an international business magazine .

He is a trustee of The Walnut Street Theater, the oldest English-speaking theater in the world, and Cheyney University, the oldest African American University in the United States. Marc has a Master's degree in Management from Penn State University and a B.S. in journalism from West Virginia University.

Chapter Key Points

- The ability to write a clear, concise, and substantive proposal is important both to getting the client and to outlining the relationship so there will be no misunderstandings.

- When developing a proposal, remember to do the following:

- Listen and take notes about what the prospective client wants.

- Read back to the client what your understanding is of what they want.

- Develop a draft proposal and present the draft in person.

- Show the client the changes you made in the redrafted proposal.

- Review your fee.

BUILDING A STAFF

Some people become consultants because they don't want the responsibility of having to manage and support employees financially and mentally. Others want to build a business with employees because they enjoy managing people, because they want to build equity in something that can be sold, or so that they can go on vacation and know that money is still coming in.

It's virtually impossible to sell a one- or two-person consulting practice unless the practice has long-term contracts and the work is unique enough that the person buying the practice has the same expertise. Even with those qualifiers, many clients may want to cancel the contracts because they don't have a relationship with the new buyer or are uncomfortable with the new buyer.

Pros and Cons of Hiring Help

There are pros and cons to building a consulting practice with staff. You should consider having full-time or semi-dedicated independent contractors for the following reasons:

Ongoing Revenue: Every time you go on vacation, unless you bring billable work with you, you are giving up an opportunity to earn money. When you have employees and they are busy, you are making money while sunning yourself at a tropical resort.

Ability to Parcel Out Work: Having employees means you can delegate work to other people while you strategize with existing clients and prospect for new clients. It's easier to maintain your creative juices if you can off-load work to other people. One-person consulting operations tend to burn out eventually.

Increased Capabilities: No person can be a master of all things. Therefore, having full- or part-time employees increases the variety of services you can offer clients; that, in turn, can attract new clients and, possibly, retain existing clients.

Potential to Attract Bigger Clients: Most big companies are much more comfortable hiring large consulting firms because they like the depth and range of experiences a firm with multiple employees has. They get a warm feeling knowing that, if a project requires more resources, the consulting firm on the project can bring more human assets to fulfill those needs.

Increased Deal Flow: If you train your employees well, they can all be out selling the firm's capabilities, which can generate new revenue.

Something to Sell: If you have full-time employees, you have a business to sell. Companies and individuals like to buy companies with full-time employees because, in most

Many large corporations become very nervous when they have to deal with a one-person operation because they are concerned that, if something happens to that person, then their project won't get done. Having some depth of talent, such as five to ten people, can often convince a large company that their financial and time investment working with a consultant will not be in jeopardy and will pay off.

cases, the employees have jelled together to form a competent team, the cost of recruiting and training has already been absorbed, and, depending on the industry, the buyer will acquire people with hard-to-come-by skills.

You might not want full-time, part-time, or even independent contractors for various reasons. Here are six things to consider before retaining the first person to work with you:

Requires Constant Feeding: Anyone who is married and is the sole breadwinner knows what it is like to have to make payroll. I have had many experiences running companies with as few as three employees and as many as 50. I enjoyed building a successful team, but what I didn't like was the day-in and day-out pressure of having to bring in enough revenue to support everyone and relying on other people. Right now, I handle projects ranging from $5,000 to $15,000. Occasionally, I have the need for a specific type of expert, whom I will bring in. I don't mind bringing in independent contractors for specific projects, but I don't want to have to worry about continually bringing in new clients to support full- or part-time people.

Managing Personalities: Being an owner of a business with employees is similar to being the patriarch or matriarch in a family. You need to be a psychologist, a disciplinarian, and a cheerleader to motivate and cajole adults into playing together and doing what you want. I can't count all of the times that business associates who have employees have lamented to me that they wish the only thing they had to do was work with clients. You really have to enjoy molding, shaping, and improving people if you are going to have employees.

Roller Coaster of Hiring/Firing: I don't know too many people who enjoy spending time reviewing resumes, hiring, and training people. I know even fewer people who enjoy having to let people go, especially if the only reason is because you can't afford to feed them any longer. I have friends who have built successful consulting practices end up in the emergency wards at hospitals from anxiety attacks related to firing people during a downturn in their business.

Benefits/Taxes: Paying for one's own benefits is expensive, but having to pay salaries to several people and offer them competitive benefits such as vacation, sick days, and retirement, plus their Social Security and unemployment tax costs, is enough to cause a major migraine.

Office Equipment/Travel: Let's not forget that you need to supply your employees with computers, telephones, business supplies, and office space. Does signing equipment and real-estate leases excite you or make you wish you never moved out of your basement office?

Marketing Costs: When you are a one-person consulting firm, you can buy business cards, possibly have a brochure, develop an inexpensive Web site, and, on rare occasions, hire a public relations consultant to send out press releases. Or, once a year you might send out a mailer.

If you are still bent on building an organization, consider the experiences of two highly successful people who have built successful organizations. I interviewed Richard Anthony, Sr., who built a virtual consulting practice, and Bill Schnell, who has built a sizable consulting firm made up of full-time employees.

Virtual Consulting Practice

Richard J. Anthony, Sr., has been a consultant and counselor on human-resource management and performance improvement to more than a generation of business leaders

> *O nce you have employees, you need to develop and fund a serious marketing plan or you won't be able to bring in the revenue to support your organization.*

and managers. He is founder and managing director of The Solutions Network, Inc., a management consulting firm based in Villanova, PA; and founder and executive director of the Center for Privately Held Companies, a forum for executives of private companies; and co-founder and co-chairperson of iGrandparents.com, an acclaimed Web site for the 70 million grandparents in the United States. He is also a member of several for-profit and not-for-profit boards. He holds an A.B. from Villanova University, attended Saint Joseph's University and Temple University for graduate study in business and organizational communication, and completed an advanced management program at Harvard University.

Question: Why did you start a virtual consulting practice?

Response: I started in 1994, after 23 years in the HR consulting business and having worked for two of the biggest and one of the best—Towers Perrin. I saw too many service firms that built monuments to themselves and they spent money on things like technology and buildings that didn't make sense.

I wanted to be lean and mean. I wasn't sure I wanted a bricks-and-mortar business. I witnessed myself the mistakes companies were making, limiting themselves in terms of the experience and competencies of the staff.

With virtual consultancy, I wouldn't be limited because I could develop a core group and then a vast network of people I met over the years. The other thing I wanted was not to have the burden of bricks and mortar and infrastructure. When I started this, it was easy to do because so many talented people were available for a variety of reasons, ranging from loss of jobs to wanting to be out on their own.

The technology was available to create and hold a network together and manage the assignment. The whole notion of a virtual consultancy was more acceptable to the market. Finally, I believe in my market, which is New York, Eastern Pennsylvania, and Baltimore, and I wanted to set up an alternative to traditional consulting firms. We allowed the client to plug into a very experienced network of consultants. We are a one-call, full-service consultancy specializing in human resource-management and performance improvement.

Question: What are the positives of having contract employees?

Response: It's principally cost and flexibility. Each affiliate also has a network of contacts to collaborate with us, which increases our visibility. I don't go to bed worried about paying other people's bills. They are independent businesspeople. We do the marketing for them if they and we are able to match experience with client fit.

Question: What is the downside of having contract employees?

Response: They have to give Solutions contracts priority and they have to fly our flag, but at the end of the day you don't have full control as if they were full-time employees.

Question: Do you find contract employees work harder or better than full-time employees do?

Response: I don't think they work harder, but the really good ones are good marketers. A good independent consultant has to be disciplined and tends to work smarter in terms of use of time and resources because they don't have the large company resources behind them. Independent consultants are willing to do a variety of things because they don't have junior people available to drive it down to.

Question: If you want to sell your business, is there any value in having contract employees?

Response: I don't think there is any value to a prospective buyer if I don't exist. There is no recurring revenue stream, no products, and no intellectual property. We have a client list, but there is no inherent economic value.

Question: How long are contracts typically, and what percentage do you take?

Response: We have a contract with Evergreen and it lasts until they or I decide it is over. Depending on the contract, what I take can range from 20 percent up to 33 percent. I played with a lot of formulas and it seemed fair because of the marketing effort involved and because of the project management responsibility. If an affiliate brings in a deal, then the percentage is lower than if I bring the deal to the affiliate.

Question: Can they work for competitors?

Response: Yes! If they work for too many competitors, the market can be confused.

Question: Is there a cost to having contract employees?

Response: The cost is in keeping the network vibrant and fresh. I do lose money because I am not billing. The trade is the contractor gives us a wholesale rate and we work hard to find good contracts that will leverage their skill sets and experience.

Question: What are the tax advantages of having contract employees?

Response: I don't have to pay withholding taxes, benefits, paid vacations, or administrative costs.

Question: Does it bother clients that your employees aren't full-time?

Response: In seven years, I have only been in one situation where a client was uneasy because the employees weren't salaried. I reassured the client that there is a lot of job-hopping and moving with salaried employees. Our contractors have made a conscious decision to be full-time consultants and greatly value the relationships.

Question: What is the one piece of advice you would give someone starting a virtual consulting business?

Response: If you come from a large corporation, it takes time to get used to not having resources. You need to know what you want in terms of the business environment, what you want from the people you work with, and you need to stay flexible as business situations change and evolve. You have to remember you are a businessperson first and an expert at whatever you do for consulting second. That means you have to operate your practice like the businesses you worked for in order to be successful.

Going the Traditional Route: Hiring Full-Time Employees

Bill Schnell is the founder/CEO of Innovative Consulting Group, an 80-plus employee information-technology consulting firm with almost $10 million in sales. I met Bill in 1988 when he was a programmer for a Pittsburgh-based company called Mallet Software. In the late 1970s and into the mid-1980s, many people became computer programmers without going to college. Bill got his training working for pharmaceutical and small software companies. By the end of 1989, Bill decided to go out on his own and, within a short period of time, he decided he'd rather build a company with full-time employees than remain a one-person operation.

Question: Why did you become a consultant?

Response: Because I always wanted to own a company. I wanted to be on an invoice, not a paycheck. It also was a quick way for me to learn about business. The whole reason I went out as an independent was not to be a consultant, but to build a company. As a single consultant you can only make so much money because you only have so many hours to sell. Another reason is because a friend of mine and I were out to dinner back in 1989. My friend said he was making $35,000 (and I was making $30,000) and he said he wanted to get to $50,000 (and I thought, with five percent raises it will take forever).

Question: How much money did it take to start your consulting practice?

Response: It didn't cost me anything. I was at the right place at the right time at McNeil Pharmaceutical. I was managing a small project and the project grew to 30 people and I was able to hire people into it. I was pretty well networked. I had about 18 people working for me in the first three months.

Question: Did you write a business plan for yourself?

Response: I had a formal business plan for another venture and I scaled that down for myself and Innovative. In my first company, I lost a lot of money, but my current company took off and I paid that debt off quickly.

Question: How long have you been a consultant?

Response: I actually incorporated in 1990, and I put it in play as a real company in 1993.

Question: Why did you hire full-time employees instead of making them contractors?

Response: I wanted to build a service company. I didn't want to be a body shop. We have our own ways of doing different things. Our concept requires a team approach: the players are used to working together and using our processes. Sometimes we hire independents to fill gaps.

Question: What is the best part of being a consultant?

Response: I believe the best part is helping your client by providing a service they can't get from within. I always thrived on providing knowledge about technology that clients don't know. I like the variety of projects. I like the art of always creating, whether it's an application or a business.

Question: What is the worst part of being a consultant?

Response: The worst part is, when the market is soft, you are the first to be pushed out. I would say some organizations usually don't know how to use consultants. They use them like they would contractors, who do what you tell them and get paid by the hour. A consultant is a partner and clients forget that. Sometimes consultants are used for political reasons, which may be to justify something the top management wants to do to avoid infighting.

Question: What is the hardest part of being a consultant?

Response: The hardest part is staying abreast or ahead of your customer's knowledge about what you do. A lot of consultants aren't proactive in terms of staying ahead of the client's needs. Travel is a problem because you don't know where the next assignment is. You are there to make the client look successful and there are consultants who forget they are there to make the client successful, not themselves.

Question: What do you like best about what you do?

Response: I like the position I am in terms of providing a high-end service that impacts their return on investment. I like to create and build. I like knowing I make a difference with my client. Consulting gives me a chance to express myself in many different ways.

Question: What do you like least about what you do?

Response: The people management. I like leading people, but not managing them. I don't have time in my schedule to hold them accountable. I like to create an environment to help them grow. I can mentor, but I don't like managing by accountability.

Question: How did you figure what to charge your clients?

Response: We are a regional company and we try to be the best in our region. I follow what the national guys charge and try to stay under their rate structure.

Question: How did you get your first client?

Response: My first client was McNeil Pharmaceutical and I was working with Coopers & Lybrand.

Question: How do you market and sell yourself?

Response: I used my existing network; the second level was hiring salespeople. Once we expanded, we built on our personal network. A lot of our vendors bring us in to work with their clients. We just started doing direct mail. We have written white papers and sent out company newsletters.

Question: How much experience do you think someone needs before going out and becoming a consultant?

Response: You need a broad foundation. You need a good understanding of business and the lifecycle of the development of a business, as well as techniques around sales. Most people know their trade, but they don't how to operate at different levels in the corporation. You need to be well read and well spoken; you need to pay attention to your appearance, and, I would say, a minimum of five years of experience, if you are in the technology field, and maybe a little longer in other fields. You need to understand the hurdles ahead of you and how to deal with them.

Question: How long did it take you until you were making the same salary and benefits you had when you were employed by someone else?

Response: It happened immediately. I didn't take any loss. I actually had started another company and had incurred a lot of debt, but my consulting took off. I wiped out my debt and made as much as I did working for someone. After that I made more. Now I live off of other people's work.

Question: Do you ask for a retainer before you do your work and, if so, how much?

Response: No! We bill people anywhere from weekly to monthly, depending on the project.

Question: Have you ever had a client who refused to pay and, if so, what did you do?

Response: Yes! I have one right now. I am turning it over to a collection agency. I tend to try to work it out with the client first and offer to put them on a payment plan.

Appraise Yourself

The last thing you need to do before you start building a business that supports more than yourself is to make an honest assessment of your skills as a manager and leader. I know a lot of people who fancy themselves empire builders, but fall short in the following 10 critical areas that lead to catastrophe.

Vision: Bill Schnell said the most important attribute of building a consulting practice that supports others is having a vision of where you want to go and being able to communicate that vision. While I was writing this book, one of my clients called me and asked if I could meet him for dinner. He proceeded to tell me that after the terrorist bombing on September 11, 2001, his business dropped off so severely that he laid off 75 percent of his 100-person workforce. Much to my surprise, he was neither panicked nor depressed. He didn't call me for advice; he called tell me about the new vision for his company and how excited he was. The flipside of this was another former client who watched his business slip from 80 people to five and said he would never want the responsibility of having to bring in enough money to support someone other than himself.

Planning: The most successful consultants I know write a business plan for themselves and then look at it once a year or every other year. When you are building a business that encompasses more than just you, you have to constantly develop plans that you can share with your team so everyone knows where the business is going.

Listening: Some consultants are great at listening to their clients, but they don't listen to their employees. You have to listen and prove you are listening by implementing the ideas of your employees or you won't be able to keep them.

Delegating: There are people who either don't trust others to fulfill assignments, have a hard time letting go and want to handle all of the details themselves, or are afraid that other people's mistakes will cost them money. You can't attract and keep talent if you won't let them take ownership and responsibility. One of my clients built a very suc-

No Plan, No Business

One of my clients was a terrific salesman, but a poor planner. When the market for his service declined, he had no plan in place to drive the business. His best employees asked him what his plan was to move the business in the right direction and he only stared at them. The best people started to put out their resumes and within a year he was in bankruptcy.

cessful IT consulting practice during the 1990s when IT services were in hot demand. Unfortunately, he could never keep managers because he constantly meddled and took away their decision-making authority. Finally, his secretary came to him and said the business would sink quickly because of his micromanaging. Much to his credit, he hired an executive coach and gradually let his managers manage. His team came up with new revenue opportunities and the business survived and is prospering.

Eye for Talent: You need to have the skills to recognize ability and potential in others. The best business builders are those who look for people who are smart, bring complementary skills, are creative, and could run the business in their place. A guy who was a major micromanager once brought me in to turn around a business. What impressed me the most about this client was his ability to attract talent. His problem was the next skill on my list.

Coexisting with Talent: Because some people need to show others that they are smarter and better, they need to compete constantly.

Fiscal Discipline: One of my best clients, who has built three successful public companies, always reminds me that the best entrepreneurs are those who respect money. That means, if you are in a business in which few of your customers ever come to visit you, don't waste money on expensive office space. If you don't pick up your customers for lunch, then don't buy expensive cars. I am a big believer in building up cash reserves that would allow a business to run a year without bringing in any money.

Coaching: Good leaders and managers enjoy making others better around them. Just because you are great at coaching clients doesn't mean that you like or would be good at

> *My client, who was good at picking talent, had no skills at coexisting with talent because he needed to show them he was better than they were. This juvenile behavior wore thin and his best people and clients began to leave.*

coaching your own employees on a day-to-day basis. If you like coaching people on a daily basis and watching them improve, having employees will be fun and rewarding. Look at the best people and coaches you have admired: the one thing they have in common is that they get excited and fulfilled by watching others succeed because of the help they have provided.

Calm: Through good times and bad you must always maintain an outward appearance of calm. Employees, like children, take their cue from you. If you are panicked, hypersensitive, or moody, employees will lose trust and faith in you. I had a client who was a visionary and a good salesperson, but she had a negative characteristic that undermined everything she did. She wasn't approachable when she was having a bad day or things weren't going well.

Communication Skills: The most important skill you can have in running an organization is the ability to communicate verbally and in writing what you want to accomplish, how you want things done, giving praise, and critiquing people. The leader who has poor communication skills will find it difficult to attract and retain good people.

Ask others for feedback and decide for yourself whether you have the skills, experience, mental makeup, and stomach to build an organization. It is much harder to feed 5, 10, or 20 people than it is to feed one.

Chapter Key Points

🔑 One of the major reasons people become consultants is because they don't want the hassle and aggravation of managing people. There are others, such as the two men I interviewed for this chapter, Bill Schnell and Richard Anthony, who wanted to develop consulting practices that didn't rely on their ability to bring in new business and develop and execute projects. Both have been very successful, even in the tough business climate we are in as I write this book.

🔑 Before you begin building a practice that requires you to support other people, write down the positive aspects of hiring people, such as:

- ongoing revenue
- ability to parcel out work
- increased capabilities
- potential to attract bigger clients
- increased work possibilities
- something to sell

🔑 Then put down the negative aspects (and you may think of other things besides what I have listed), such as:

- require constant feeding
- need to manage personalities
- roller-coaster of hiring/firing
- paying benefits/taxes
- providing office equipment/travel
- marketing costs

🔑 Now write down what you and other people perceive as your greatest attributes as a leader and manager, such as:

- your vision for your company
- your ability to plan
- your ability to listen to others
- your willingness to delegate to others
- an eye for talent
- your ability to coexist with talent
- the quality of fiscal discipline
- your ability and willingness to coach others
- a calm approach to crises
- communication skills

Finally, write out what your personal and professional short-term goals are and then decide if you really want the pressure of hiring, firing, and supporting other people.

PARTNERSHIPS

SHARING THE WEALTH—AND THE WORK ◀

B ecause many people don't like working alone, they look for a partner. They want a partner for any number of good reasons, ranging from having someone to talk to about aspirations and problems to helping to sell their services. I have to admit that being a sole practitioner is a lonely business. I recently started a new venture with my wife and it's nice to have someone to strategize with, complain to, commiserate with, and share the workload.

I have tried having informal partnerships with people to get a sense of what it would be like to work with someone else. It's just as difficult to find a good partner as it is to find the right spouse. Some of the people I have partnered with are good technically, but are slow to complete their work, or they are poor hunters and are not good at bringing in new business.

Ten Criteria for Selecting a Partner

Before you decide to work with a friend or look for partners, you should develop a set of criteria for the type of person with whom you would be comfortable working. The following list will help you identify your best choice for a partner.

1. Ability to Bring in Clients. It's nice to have a partner who has good sales skills so all of the pressure to bring in clients isn't on one person. I worked with someone who had excellent technical skills, but was not interested or good at bringing in new clients. I personally didn't like having all the pressure on me to support two people's salaries. I needed someone who could pull his or her own weight.

2. Good Writing Skills. Consulting professionals have to have good writing skills because clients expect quality reports that they can share with subordinates and superiors.

3. Good Verbal Communication Skills. It's important that a partner be able to present you as well as you would represent yourself. Good verbal skills inspire confidence in clients.

4. Detail Oriented. Some people are good at getting the project, but are poor at delivering quality work because they don't pay attention to the details. In consulting, paying attention to the details is everything. I once worked with someone I was considering asking to partner with me. She was bright, well-educated, and experienced. I asked her to edit a business plan for me and she told she edited it. I didn't review her work and the client found numerous errors. Unfortunately, this was the third time this had happened and one of my clients strongly suggested I never use this person again.

> *One of my colleagues went into business with a former client who was knowledgeable, but not good at bringing in business. The partnership died within six months because my colleague became frustrated about having to feed two mouths and still do the work.*

5. Good at Multitasking. Most consultants have worked for a large company and are used to having a variety of people handle different tasks for them. In a startup consulting business, you have to be good at multitasking because you don't have a legion of support staff. A friend of mine went into partnership with a very experienced man from a *Fortune* 1000 company. The problem wasn't with the partner's knowledge or ability to deliver a quality result, but he wasn't used to doing things for himself and looked to outsource many of the administrative tasks. This was a drain on time and money, and my friend eventually split up the partnership.

6. Handles Pressure Well. There is a lot of pressure in consulting. I have lost a lot of sleep over proposals that were not accepted, or going for months with no income, or clients who make me wish I had never become a consultant. The greatest pressure is in bringing in revenue. Many people are enamored with the allure of being their own bosses and, in many cases, working out of their homes. But when business doesn't come in and their bank accounts begin to shrink, they will want to find a safe job. I know, because that fear has hit many of my friends who jumped in and out of consulting.

7. Good Follow-Up Skills. One of my clients was in partnership with a man who was terrific at getting first meetings and making a good first impression, but he was poor at following up with prospective clients if they didn't respond right away. He lost a lot of good prospects and, after a couple of years, he ended up in the emergency ward of the hospital because the stress of following up and getting new business affected his health.

8. Good Networking Skills. Part of networking is the ability to bring in new clients, but a bigger part of networking is developing contacts who will open doors to new business. I had a friend who wanted to go into partnership with me, so we worked together for a year. For the entire year, I asked him repeatedly to go to various functions and make contacts for us to get new business. Every time an event came up, he had an excuse why he couldn't go. I got tired of being the sole source for making contacts and bringing in opportunities.

9. Database of Contacts. The hardest part of starting a consulting practice is getting clients. If you are going into partnership with someone, you want to know they have a robust database of business contacts that could lead to business.

10. Ability to Interact with High-Level Professionals. The ability to feel comfortable and interact with people at a high level is important because many consulting opportunities come from the vice president to CEO level because of the high rates consultants have to charge for their work. A client of mine took on a partner who got tongue-tied when he interacted with high-level people. All my client's partner's ideas seemed weak and ineffectual because he was so intimidated.

Starting a Partnership

I interviewed Azriela Jaffe about what it takes to build a successful partnership. Azriela has an M.B.A. and a B.S.W. and is the founder of Anchored Dreams (www.createyourown-luck.com) and author of *Let's Go into Business Together: Eight Secrets for Successful Business Partnering* (CareerPress, 2001). She also writes a weekly column for *Netscape Business/Fortune Magazine Online*, called "Balancing Act." She lives in Yardley, PA, with her husband and three children.

Question: What is the best way to evaluate whether I should work on my own or partner with someone?

Response: Take a look at your past history. Beware the partner who has a tale of woe about how every partner in their previous business life has been a loser, and if only they could find the right partner, everything would be golden. Maybe some fourth or fifth marriages work, but wouldn't you be skittish if you were his or her fifth spouse? Some people can't partner well with anyone, but rather than owning responsibility for this fact, they blame their business partnership failures on a string of bad-luck partners. Maybe they are the source of the bad luck!

Question: What is the best way to evaluate someone I am thinking of starting a business with?

Response: Take the time to get to know him or her. I'm startled at the number of business partnerships, involving serious risk, money, and emotional investment, that start after the equivalent of having a first date or two. It's no different than eloping and going to the altar after only a few dates at the movies. If you want to move quickly, you are apt to overlook some of the deficits in your prospective partner because you are so eager to receive the perceived benefits.

Talk with previous business partners, employees, friends, his or her spouse—anyone who can give you a clue on how this person operates, in business and outside. Check the individual's credit history—you have a legitimate reason to if money is at stake. Make sure that your personalities click and that this is someone with whom you feel you can resolve conflict. Bottom line: is this someone you respect and trust?

Question: What personal qualities and characteristics should you look for when selecting a partner?

> *D*o an honest inventory of your personality and assess whether you are ready to share power and control and to delegate responsibility to someone else for running some aspect of your company. Many people want the benefits of partnership without the risks and challenges that come along with it.

Forewarned Is Forearmed

A friend of mine worked part-time as a consultant for a small software company. The owner was a good salesperson, but not much of a technologist. My friend was invited to be a partner to head up technology. He was given 25 percent of the company. Over the first year, the partnership seemed to work fine, but when he went to apply for a mortgage for a new house, he found out that his partner hadn't been paying the taxes and that he owed $50,000. Needless to say, the partnership blew up and my friend spent seven years paying off the debts.

Response: Be sure to partner with someone who has complementary skills that fill in the gaps in your background and experience. If you partner with someone just like yourself, it might feel more comfortable, but it won't help your business much. Also, remember that this is an intimate relationship, and so, just as in marriage, you should look for the personal characteristics of trustworthiness, integrity, courteousness, ability to handle stress and conflict, and someone who is not threatened by your abilities and success. Check out the motivations and motives of your business partners. What are they looking to get out of this business partnership with you, and is that goal in sync with yours?

Question: What types of skills should one look for in a partner?

Response: Whatever you are missing in your business or whatever you know you are weak in and could use some strengthening in. Remember, your partner doesn't have to be well skilled in everything—are you? Also, it may not be skills you are looking for. It might be financial investment, or contacts, or prestige and a good reputation in a particular industry you are trying to enter. The skill that any partner should have, however, is the ability to partner!

Question: Should we both put in an equal amount of money?

Response: Absolutely not a criterion. In fact, many partnerships are formed with a legal understanding that one partner is the majority investor, or that one person will put in the money and the other put in the skills, or some other division of labor and money. The key is that both parties agree on what is a fair ownership share of the company, given initial investment. Also, be careful of partnerships where one person is putting in all of the money and the other is putting in all the time. In the long run, it can work, but often, if the company gets into trouble, the partners start finger-pointing about who the problem is. Ideally, even if not equal, all partners will have some financial investment. Otherwise, the one who is merely putting in his or her time will find it easier to walk away.

Question: Should we both put in the same amount of time?

Response: Likewise per above, this is not necessary at all, as long as both partners are fairly compensated. Be aware that the number-one fight business partners have is over time and the perception that one is working harder than the other is or not hard enough. So, this issue about who will work how much time and how it will be measured should be discussed regularly. When the company is in trouble, partners can blame it on a partner not working hard enough. When the company is doing well, partners can claim that each is working harder than the other is and, therefore, should be compensated more than the other is. So, be sure you have an objective measure of time invested.

Question: Should we write out a letter of understanding that describes what we expect from each other and sign it?

Response: Yes, absolutely, even if it's written on a loose-leaf piece of paper and not drawn up by an attorney. Any kind of written understanding is better than none at all.

Question: What are the most common conflicts partners have?

Response: As I mentioned above, arguments about who is working the hardest and where the fault lies when a company is troubled are the ones that occur most often. Also, conflicts in work style and communication also occur frequently in personal relationships. Sometimes it feels as if your business partner is from a different planet! Also, partners may argue about the overall vision and long- or short-term goals for the company and how best to achieve them.

Question: What percentage of partnerships fails?

Response: No one really knows for sure. You'll hear dreadful statistics like as much as 50 to 80 percent. Suffice it to say, it's a high enough number that you should approach business partnership cautiously.

Question: What are the biggest mistakes people make when going into a partnership?

Response: Leaping without looking, going into it desperately, and not really knowing who they are "marrying," and then discovering that their so-called hero is really a jerk. Also, underestimating how much a business partnership relationship mirrors a marriage and how much emotional investment it will take to make this intimate relationship work.

Husband-and-Wife Partnerships

I know a lot of husbands and wives who go into business together. The criteria you apply to nonspouses should be applied to spouses because a lot more is at risk than your business partnership. Your marriage could become strained or even unravel. Couples that partner often have a difficult time of being brutally honest with each other and then, when problems arise, they don't confront them and both the partnership and the marriage fail.

I interviewed Karen and Don Kaufman, who founded the Kaufman Partnership in 1979. The firm specializes in impression management for executives, professionals, and entrepreneurs. Over the past 20 years they have coached and trained over 2,000 people. They have been quoted in *The Wall Street Journal,* the *Los Angeles Times,* and other major publications. Both Karen and Don have master's degrees in Organizational Dynamics from the University of Pennsylvania. Karen and Don provide insights concerning what it takes for couples to build successful partnerships.

Question: Why did you go into business together?

Response: I had sold my mortgage company and was looking for something to do. My wife, Karen, had started a business as a personal fashion consultant and I, of course, offered some suggestions on how she should promote her business and get it off the ground. I never realized at the time that I was fulfilling a fantasy I had of being in business with my wife. I always admired show business couples and thought they enjoyed working together, but I never knew what form the business might take, and I certainly would not have picked fashion consulting; that didn't seem manly enough. But I was intrigued with the concept and pushed my way into Karen's little business.

Question: Did you put together a business plan?

Response: No! Not really. Today I can look back and tell you we were always involved in organizations and projects we had an interest in and met a lot of people we liked and who began to use our services. We call it productive participation.

Question: How long have you been working together?

Response: We have been working together since 1980. We have been married since 1973.

Question: What is the best part of working together?

Response: The best part is that we have a common purpose and project and it gives us lots to talk about. Literally everything we do is brought into the business. We went to graduate school together, took up golf together, and are interested in people and how they relate to each other, especially in organizations. But the best part is always having someone to talk to when you need to discuss a client or business problem.

Question: What is the most difficult part of working together?

Response: Scheduling dinner at night. When we first started working together, we had to get over sibling rivalry. It forced us to become more mature in our interactions with each other. Some of that is brought on by a certain amount of role reversal and defining roles became an important part of our interaction. Once we defined roles, we cooperated much better.

Question: How do you divide up your duties?

Response: We made a list of all the things that go on in the business. Then we listed what each of us does and laid them out in terms of roles and responsibilities. We also included our administrative staff and another consultant we have. By defining the roles, we could see how the work as distributed between us as well. We even broke it down by percentages so we could get a handle on it. Karen was stronger in sales and I focused on marketing. We both have clients and we distribute them by gender or by issue.

Question: How do you avoid 24-hour shoptalk?

Response: We have specific rules. We decided there would be no shoptalk in the bedroom. At dinner we will recap the day discussing business and recreation plans for the weekend. On the weekends we play golf and there is no room for business.

Question: If you have a dispute, how do you settle it?

Response: We have an outside coach who works with us every two weeks and we work on our development: some is client-focused and some is relationship-focused. Coaching helps us to be more objective and to see through our personality stuff, which can get in the way of a productive relationship.

Question: What is the biggest mistake you have made as a team and how did you fix it?

Response: I think it was when we formed the company. We had a large number of consultants working for us. We spent more time managing than developing the concept and that took us off track. We fixed it by getting rid of everyone and regrouped. We had a retail location, which was another mistake, and we had to regroup and swallow the bullet and our pride. We work out of our home now, keep expenses to a minimum, and see clients in their offices or in one of the private clubs we belong to. Our support staff is virtual, many of them home-based as well.

Question: What is the one piece of advice you would give a husband and wife who are considering going into business together?

Response: Have a good relationship going in and respect each other and make sure you have a good advisor; don't try to do it all yourself. Finally, have an objective outside coach who will not take sides. Most importantly, love what you're doing.

Partnership Agreement

Once you have decided with whom you want to partner, you need to develop a partnership agreement. The initial agreement can be developed by you and your intended partner(s), but the final document should be developed by an attorney in order to make sure it conforms with the laws of the state in which you work and form the partnership. The agreement should include the following points:

Stock Allocation. When you start a partnership, you have to incorporate the business. Most partnerships form a limited liability partnership, which allows for a division of profits and expenses between the partners. The partners have to decide if it's a 50–50 division of company stock or if one partner is going to get more stock than the other. Stock allocation can be determined by how much more one partner is investing over the other or who has the title and responsibilities of president or managing partner. I had a friend who created a formula based on the amount of sales each partner brought in and then looked at a running average over a three-year period to determine the amount of stock each person owned.

Profit Allocation. Everyone thinks that the amount of stock determines the amount of profits each partner receives. One of my clients brought in a partner who was a terrific rainmaker and, although he wasn't a large shareholder, he was granted more of the profits because the other partners saw their salaries and bonuses grow.

Salaries. Before you get started, you need to determine the amount of salary each person will receive. The formula may be based on revenue projected to be brought in or the amount of company stock or a combination of both.

Benefits. A friend of mine was discussing entering into a partnership with someone and the deal breaker turned out to be the benefits package. My friend's spouse worked for a company with great benefits and his partner's spouse was an at-home mother. The partner needed benefits, which wasn't a problem, but it was the type, level, and cost of the benefits my friend objected to. They couldn't get over this issue and decided to part company.

Vacation. Many people who go into a partnership don't even think about deciding on what constitutes an acceptable amount of vacation. They just figure each partner will take vacation as they need it, but will put the business before vacations. One of my clients didn't define the amount of vacation each partner could take, and in the first year her partner took four weeks to her one week. During those four weeks, my client had to cover for her partner and, at the end of the year, the partner still wanted the same amount of bonus. My client said it wasn't fair and the partner pointed out that it was her choice not to take more vacation. The partnership survived because they agreed to define how much vacation each partner could take, and each partner had to take the vacation whether she needed it or not.

Cash Investment. Some partners start out with one partner putting up all the money and others start out with some type of split. There is no hard-and-fast rule. The person who may be willing to put up all of the money initially may be willing to sell stock over time or just give stock to the other partner because of the partner's capabilities.

Problem Resolution. Just as in a marriage, there will be times when you can't resolve your differences and you need to decide how conflicts will be resolved. I advise clients to bring in an outside person to listen to both sides and make suggestions on how to reach a compromise. Don't let problems fester and destroy the partnership.

Company Breakup. At some point, one partner may want to leave or one partner may want to break up the partnership. You need to have a plan in place that determines how one side can buy out the other's stock and over what period of time.

Titles. I have seen partnerships crash before they got off the ground because of arguments over titles. One partner wants the title of president or managing partner and the other doesn't think either partner should have perceived control over the other.

Responsibilities and Duties. A list of responsibilities should be developed and agreed on. There will be a lot of resentment if one partner is totally responsible for accounting and bill paying and the other partner is only responsible for bringing in his or her share of business and working on his or her own projects.

Chapter Key Points

🔑 Partnerships can be great because you don't have to rely only on yourself to bring in clients or do the work.

🔑 Before you take on a partner, however, make sure you take time to do the following:

- Develop a list of the characteristics you want in a partner.
- Work with someone for a predetermined period before making a decision.

- Be sure that your skills and personalities are complementary.
- Make sure that you can live with that individual on a daily basis.
- Discuss and put in writing a partnership agreement that both of you can live with.

Make sure your personalities and skill sets are complementary. Think of a partnership like a marriage and make sure you can live with that person from day to day.

Define and discuss a partnership agreement that each side can live with.

CHAPTER 14

PROTECTING YOURSELF FROM CROOKED CLIENTS

DEALING ONLY WITH HONEST PEOPLE ◀

E very consultant I interviewed for this book and practically all the ones I've known over the years don't mind going after new business, love meeting new people, feel a great sense of self-worth after providing a service that will make a difference, and thoroughly enjoy their work.

No one, however, likes having to collect money and dealing with dishonest and/or unreasonable clients. I can't tell you how many times I wish I had a tough relative to collect fees owed to me. Over the past decade, I have learned a lot about how best to protect myself and increase my chances of collecting what is owed to me.

Ten Personalities to Avoid

When you start your consulting practice, be on the lookout for the following types of personalities among your clients:

1. Finger Pointer: Most people recognize that it is rare for one party to be completely at fault for something, yet there are people who refuse to take responsibility if things go wrong. According to them, everyone else is at fault, but they aren't. They always look for a scapegoat.

One of my clients was an international company that provided access to a variety of databases to health-care organizations. They hired a Web-site consulting firm that delivered a product that didn't meet their expectations.

When I was brought in by the CIO to fix the project, I asked him what organization had run the project that I was taking over and who in that organization was responsible. It turned out that the fired vendor was made up of the best employees from my old company. I called those employees to ask them what happened, and they told me the mistakes they had made and where they felt the client fell short.

I asked them if they had spoken to the CEO about what they thought wasn't happening on the client's end, and they said "yes," but the CEO refused to acknowledge or even offer to look into any of their complaints. When I brought in vendors to interview who would take on the various tasks of the past vendor, the CEO spent the first 15 to 30 minutes saying negative things about the last vendor. His comments were so filled with venom that other consulting firms refused to submit a bid for fear that, if they didn't live up to the client's expectations, they, too, would have their reputations besmirched by this CEO.

2. Dreamer: There are dreamers like Thomas Edison and Steve Jobs, who have a vision of how they can change the world, and then there are dreamers who refuse to face reality and deal with it. Sometimes dreamers can con people into funding their ideas or working for the promise of payments to come later.

Once, after I spoke to an audience of entrepreneurs, one of them came up to me and said he would like to speak to me about engaging me to help him with his company. He looked serious, spoke well, and told me just enough to agree to a meeting. After 30 minutes of meeting with him, I realized his ideas were not grounded in reality and that his professional life experiences had not prepared him for what he wanted to do.

I could smell disaster in the future. Another colleague of mine agreed to work with him and, after his first payment, never saw another check and was constantly promised payment because his "concept" couldn't miss.

3. Impatient Individual: One of my clients had terrific sales skills, but his lack of personal discipline and impatience resulted in having to do things over and caused miscalculations and poor feelings among his management team. He is also a screamer, which I find to be unprofessional behavior that can undermine the success of a project. Be careful with impatient people because they will push to get a job done quickly and, when it isn't to their liking, they will blame you.

Even the Rich and Famous Can Be Problems

An associate of mine worked on a very famous television personality's Web site. The associate told the star that the site would have some glitches because the star wanted the site up quickly. The site went live and, because some sections didn't work properly, the star refused to pay. My friend took the star to court and got an out-of-court settlement that won the bulk of her money.

4. People Without Commitment: There are individuals and organizations that get excited about an idea for just enough time to hire a consultant, but won't put in the time, effort, or funds to finish a project.

I have a client who started two projects simultaneously and, after a couple of months, I could see their commitment starting to fade. The only thing worse than not finishing a project is not getting paid. If given the choice, I would rather finish than get paid because it looks better on my resume. Try to avoid clients who don't have a clear and emotional commitment to finishing a project, because you will be left feeling empty.

5. Name Dropper: When you are young and trying to make an impression, you might drop a few well-known names to people in order to build credibility, but be wary of older and seemingly seasoned people who need to mention big names in order to get you to do what they want.

A colleague of mine met a guy at a conference who said he was the former vice president of marketing for two publicly traded companies and personally knew the CEOs of three New York Stock Exchange companies.

I am a skeptical person by nature, so I suggested to my colleague that he call the secretaries of the three CEOs mentioned by his potential client and see if he actually knew them. My colleague found out that one of the three slightly remembered the person, but didn't have anything of substance to say. I told my colleague not to confront the person, just bow out gracefully.

6. Paranoid Type: I may be skeptical, but I am not paranoid, and there is a huge difference. I had a client who was bright and visionary, but wore out consultants and employees by believing that everyone was stealing, or trying to take her ideas, or trying to take advantage of her.

Consultants I knew and trusted told me the same story. The relationship would start beautifully and end in name-calling because the client felt she was being taken advantage of. To prove his honesty, one consultant paid for and took a lie detector test, and the client still refused to believe the results or honor his contract.

7. Perfectionist: There is no one more frustrating to deal with than a perfectionist. Nothing is ever right and you never can complete the project and obtain your final payment because the project isn't exactly to the client's liking.

As I write this book, I am dealing with a client whose business plan I have been working on for a year and a half. I have rewritten the same paragraph eight times and the client still isn't happy, but can't pinpoint what is wrong either. I know the right course of action is to resign from the project and move on.

8. Poor Communicator: I find it exasperating to deal with clients who don't return phone calls and e-mails and can't communicate what they don't like or how they want you to change something. The lack of courtesy is an indicator of how they treat people overall and you can be assured that they will eventually lose interest in the project, blame you for its failure, and refuse to pay part or all of your bill.

9. Client with a Poor Reputation: I am the type of person who likes to judge people for myself. I know how people can say negative things that aren't true to enhance their own professional position or standing. Yet, in consulting, your reputation is everything. Be careful whom you associate with, because your name and skills will be received positively or negatively depending on the quality of your clients.

An investment banker recently called me to do work for one of his clients. He did not receive high marks from people that I knew, but I had met him before and thought

> *I had a client in New York for whom I was developing a business plan. The client had me rewrite the executive summary five times because he didn't like how I phrased various sentences. I had my editor edit four times and he still wasn't happy. Finally, I fired him as a client. Sometimes you have to fire your clients or they will eat up all of your time and make you miserable.*

he was reasonably bright. After meeting with the person, I asked that he put everything in writing so there would be no miscommunication. He said he would and that I would receive a contract within a week. That was two years ago. He never responded to my one telephone call, which told me all I needed to know.

10. Slow Payer: Few consultants start their consultancy with such a large balance in their bank account that they don't have to worry about cash flow. Ask potential clients for a list of consulting/vendor references under the pretext of wanting to make sure you provide the quality of service they expect and, while you are talking to some of the vendors, find out how long it typically takes the client to pay. If the client won't give you the names of other vendors, run, don't walk, away.

Screening Prospective Clients

I have told you about difficult personality types to be aware of, but you need to know what questions to ask in order to determine what type of personality you are dealing with. I ask prospective clients the following questions:

1. What is the project and who will benefit from it? I like to know that my clients have a clear vision of what they want to do and accomplish. If the client isn't sure, then I become concerned that the client can't define the objectives and milestones that will tell me what I need to do to complete the project successfully.

2. What is your background? I have had clients who have embarked on projects that they knew nothing about because they were assigned to it or thought it was a good idea. The problem is, if clients know nothing about what they are doing, it is hard for them to know if what you are telling them and doing for them is correct.

I wrote a business plan to raise investor capital for a client. He had never written a business plan or run a business. I gave him examples of my work and pointed out to him that I have a process, methodology, and format that I follow with every plan. The client said he liked the work. When I submitted a draft of the plan, he wanted to change the structure of it because he had read that all the competition for venture capital meant that you had to differentiate yourself from other companies looking for capital.

I told the client that venture capital investors were concerned about too many copycat business concepts, not the structure of the plan. The client said he was working on another venture with another business plan writer and had that writer develop a more creative approach to delivering his message. I suggested to the client that we send both plans to the investment bank that introduced us and see what they said. The investment bank was horrified and embarrassed by the "more creative plan" and said they would never take a plan that was so complicated for investors to follow.

The client realized I was correct, but proceeded to argue with me over the best way to present his case. Lots of time and money were wasted. The result was that nothing ever happened with the project.

3. Why do you want to do the project? Before you take a client's money, make sure you understand his or her motivations for doing the project and that it makes good business sense. Because the client was willing to pay a substantial fee, a colleague of mine agreed to take on a project that I had turned down. I warned him that the project, in my opinion, would fail because the client didn't have a compelling enough reason to do it and that my colleague would be held accountable for its failure. Sure enough, the client's boss questioned the project and questioned the integrity of my colleague for accepting the money.

4. Is there a budget for it? Many times people would like to initiate a project, but the budget they have is too small to execute it properly, or there is no budget and the prospective client is fishing for free advice. I found this out the hard way. An information-technology director for a medium-size money manager told me his firm was interested in developing a Web site. I immediately got excited because I had done the planning and overseen the development of Web sites for other money managers.

When I asked him about the budget, he told me not to worry, that he was working on one, but that he needed me to come in to speak to the partners. I spent two hours going through my methodology for planning and developing a site, showed them what competitors were doing, and provided sample ideas of what I thought would be best for them. My contact said they wanted a proposal, but his partners didn't want to provide a budget: they feared I would come in below the budget they had in mind, and that I would raise my price to take the available money.

I asked if I could present the proposal in person and was told it was unnecessary. They asked me to e-mail it and I complied. The firm took my proposal and used their own internal developers to build the site because they didn't have a budget for developing it.

Similarly, a colleague of mine, who normally bills after he finishes a project, did a small project with a signed agreement for a $50-million company, then found out that there was no budget and that the person who retained him had no authority to negotiate with side vendors.

5. Who will be the point of contact as the project moves forward? Nothing is more frustrating than having many bosses on one project. I once ran an Internet consulting company and one of our clients was the 60th-largest bank in the United States. One day the project manager came into my office crying real tears. The client was driving her crazy because they had multiple people giving her directions and each person contradicted the other.

The client called me and told me our work was so substandard and taking so long that she was going to cancel the contract. I asked the client for a meeting and said that we both were at fault. Our mistake was not insisting on one point of contact and their mistake was having too many cooks in the kitchen. Never let a client bully you into working with multiple decision makers, no matter how much money they are willing to pay you. Dealing with multiple decision makers guarantees that you will fail because you will never make them all happy and you will be in the middle of the political wars that always ensue from dealing with multiple rulers.

6. How soon does the project have to be completed? In all my years as a consultant, I have rarely had a client tell me that he or she wasn't in a rush to complete a project. There are two reasons to ask this question. First, you want to make sure you have the time and capability to manage and execute the project so the client will consider using you again and would recommend you to others. Second, and this is just as important, you need to know that the client has realistic expectations.

7. Has anyone else attempted to do this project? A good indicator of the type of client you are getting involved with is the number of different people they have hired to do the same project. As incredible as this may sound, this unfortunately happens in the consulting business when you deal with difficult people who don't know what they want or

> *The lessons learned? Don't give too much of your valuable thinking away, and always get a signed agreement up front.*

think they know more than any expert they hire. Twice in my career, I was one of a few people hired and fired for a particular project.

An accounting firm contacted me about developing a business plan for a well-known CEO. The CEO was a world-class expert in a particular area. His weakness was in communicating his ideas on paper to raise capital. The process I use in such a situation is to develop a pre-draft business plan so the client has a sense of the content of the plan and how it is laid out. The client then takes the pre-draft and provides written instructions on the changes that he or she wants made. The next step is providing a draft for other members of the management team, interested insiders, and objective outsiders, for review and feedback.

The client read the pre-draft and determined that I was clueless about what he was trying to accomplish. My client's partner had read the same document and said I was 98 percent on the money. I told the CEO that his partner felt the pre-draft only needed a little bit of work. He proceeded to call his partner and ask him what he said and the partner confirmed my story. He tore into the partner, fired me, and hired another writer. Three writers later, he was back to me with hat in hand. I told him that I would pass. The heartache was not worth it.

My other horror story is about the time that I was brought to a client by a small boutique investment bank to rewrite a business plan. I wrote a draft and everyone was happy, except the managing partner of the firm. He didn't have a problem with the content, but he didn't like the sentence structure. After we parted ways, the associate who brought me in said I was the eighth business plan writer to work with the firm, and each time the managing partner was the consultant killer.

It's important to find out if your client is a reasonable person who works with his or her consultants or is the type of person who finds fault with everything.

8. What kind of consultants do you achieve the best results with? I like to know what type of people my clients work best with. I am a creative thinker and enjoy working with clients who allow me to come up with novel ways of approaching a problem. Some clients prefer to deal with people who don't challenge their thinking, but focus on delivering the product. Some clients prefer that you work at their offices, others prefer you to come in after their employees have left, and some require that you be available to meet on weekends. You need be honest with the client about whether your style is a match for their way of operating.

9. Do you prefer to communicate by phone, e-mail, or in person? I am the type of person who feels that face-to-face meetings are a waste of time. Most of my clients are happy to interact with me by phone and e-mail. When there is something critical to talk about that requires a face-to-face meeting, I have no problem with being wherever I need to be. However, I am always concerned about clients who require a lot of face-to-face meetings because they are time killers and they are typically the same clients who insist on a fixed-price contract. If your client requires a lot of meetings in person, you need to set some ground rules or you will find that your hourly rate will diminish greatly.

10. How do you define success for this project? Never go into any project without knowing what the client expects the end result to be. A colleague of mine developed a Web site for an insurance company. The purpose of the project, my colleague was told, was to provide information to the general public about long-term health care.

What my colleague didn't know was that her client marked success by the number of potential customers who asked for quotes on long-term care. My colleague didn't know that the site was to be a sales-lead generator, so she developed a strictly informational site. If she had known that the purpose was to attract prospects who would be sent to sales agents around the country, she would have developed a different type of Web site.

Obviously, my friend should have been told to develop a site that captured sales leads, but often clients are in such a rush to execute a project that their boss wants or to respond to a threat by another company, that they don't fully think through what they hope to accomplish with the money they invest in you.

> *Make sure you ask the client to describe exactly what results they are hoping for and focus on delivering those results.*

References

Most clients will ask you for a reference to find out if you are honest, ethical, and hardworking and can deliver what you promise. I have gotten into the practice of asking prospective clients for references, but I don't frame it that way to them because I don't want to insult them or give them the impression that I am doing them a favor by speaking with them. What I tell the prospective client is that I would like to speak with consultants they have worked with whose work they like so I can make sure that my style and process are a good fit. I have encountered few clients who have a problem with this. There are five questions I like to ask:

1. What type of project did the consultant work on? It's good to know the type and caliber of consultants the prospective client likes to hire. If you know they hire people you consider "B" teamers, then that may be an indication that they don't like to pay for quality help and may want to beat you up on fees.

2. How long did they work for the client? If a consultant worked for a client for a few months to a year or more, it's a good sign that there is stability between the consultant and the client.

3. Did they enjoy working with the client and would they work with the company again? Sometimes clients will give you the name of a consultant that they had a good experience with, but the consultant had a different take on the interaction. The consultant may have been happy with the compensation, but the overall work experience might have been less pleasant.

4. Were the client's directions clear? Many times I have worked with clients whose directions about how they wanted a project done were murky and, when I asked them for clearer directions, they smiled and said they were sure that I understood what they wanted. When I started consulting, I just went along with clients, but after having a couple of clients say they were unhappy, I made sure that I worked with people who were precise about their expectations.

5. Was the client accessible when you had questions and concerns? One of the most frustrating parts of being a consultant is that you are really an outsider with insider responsibility. But, because you aren't an employee, it's often difficult to get the attention and time of your client. A national accounting firm brought me in to develop a business plan for one of their clients, one of the foremost experts in his field and a nice person. As nice and as brilliant as he was, he was, and is to this day, the most difficult client I have ever worked with.

I would e-mail him questions, follow up with telephone calls, and even ask his assistant to set up meetings, which were always canceled at the last minute. In order to get his attention, I would call him after 9 p.m. on Sunday nights after he put his children to bed. The project took twice as long to finish as it should have. As intellectually interesting as my client was, he wasn't worth having as a client.

6. Was the client quick to respond after a milestone was met? Most consultants' payments are triggered when a project hits a milestone. Many times, milestones can only be reached after the client has been involved, either by reviewing the work or by handling an aspect of the project. I had a client who sometimes took 30 to 180 days to respond, which kept me from receiving my milestone payments. Try to avoid procrastinators and overly committed people.

7. If the client didn't like something, was he or she friendly or antagonistic? I don't like to fight with people. In fact, I try to avoid confrontation at all cost. Therefore, I don't like to work with people who feel the need to belittle others or use their consultants as sparring partners. One client I had took great delight in cursing out his consultants and employees. The ironic thing about this client was that he didn't mind if you called him the same names he called you. I was forewarned, but I found it hard to believe that a nationally known and respected man like my client could behave in such manner. I found it disconcerting to deal with him and found someone to replace me on the project.

8. How did the rest of the organization treat the consultant? Some organizations have anticonsultant cultures because they believe professionals from the outside are out to displace or embarrass them. Or, they might believe consultants are brought in by senior management to validate management's ideas and undermine full-time employees. This mistrust is caused by management's failure to be clear about why an outside consultant is being brought in and to take the time to brief employees first. One of my financial industry clients had bred such distrust with its employees over consultants that I had to resign.

9. Was the client willing to be used as a reference? It is important that a client, especially a large or well-known one, is willing to be used as a reference. The bigger the client, the more important the reference. Clients who refuse to be references, I have found, are usually difficult to please.

10. How long did it take the client to pay? Unfortunately, many clients believe you should serve as an interest-free bank. The bigger the client, the longer it usually takes to collect. A friend of mine did some work for a *Fortune* 100 medical device company and it took him 90 days and a five percent discount to get the client to pay. You need to make sure you have a champion in the company who will push your invoice through.

When dealing with large companies, build in an internal interest rate. Don't bother putting in your contract that the company will pay you one to two percent per month for paying you late, because the finance department will strike it from the contract or just ignore it.

If you can't afford to carry a large company, explain it to your contact and see what he or she can do to accommodate you. If your contact can't help you, you can either factor the receivable or just walk away.

Chapter Key Points

The advice in this chapter is probably as important as anything you will read, because you need to know how to protect yourself.

🔑 Before taking on any client, make sure you do the following:

- Ask for references.

- Ask business associates what they know about the company.

- Make sure they pay consultants within 30 to 50 days.

- Make sure the company's culture embraces outside consultants.

- Make sure the objectives and assignment are clearly spelled out.

- Avoid prospective clients who don't treat professionals with respect.

🔑 Life is short, and one of the reasons you become a consultant is to take more control over your professional life. If you can afford to walk away from a client who makes you nervous or uncomfortable, do it.

COLLECTING BAD DEBTS

GET PAID FOR YOUR WORK ◀

You have tried your best to protect yourself against crazy and unscrupulous clients. Yet, no matter how many different ways you try to screen people, you are still going to have customers who will try to take advantage of you and refuse to honor their financial commitment. In my first management position, my boss told me that contracts were made to be broken and that contracts were only as good as the people who signed them.

I have found my first boss's words to be prophetic throughout my consulting career. There have been a few times that I wish I had a friend who would take a baseball bat to a client's kneecaps. During the 15 years I have been consulting, I have compiled a Top Ten list of clients' excuses for not paying me.

Top Ten Client Reasons for Not Paying

1. "Based on my understanding of the contract, you didn't fulfill it." This doesn't happen at the beginning or middle of your work, when you have shown them what you have done and had them sign off on it. It always happens at the end.

One time I signed a contract with a client to take two-thirds of my compensation in cash and one-third in stock. The client paid me the cash and, when I asked for the stock, he told me his lawyers were putting together the stock certificates. I didn't think that was a problem, because I was on the advisory board of the company and had made some significant introductions.

Three months went by. When I asked when I could expect the certificates, the client said his new investors didn't think I deserved them and, if I took them to court, they would countersue. I told my client that he was being unfair and offered arbitration. He refused, and my attorney told me to forget it and move on because the legal costs and time wasted weren't worth it.

2. "I just don't think you delivered value." A colleague of mine developed and implemented a marketing plan for an information technology service provider. My colleague did direct mail, public relations, and broadcast e-mail, he created strategic partnerships, and he set up speaking engagements. He did all of this during the worst lull in IT history and in the aftermath of the September 11th terrorists' destruction of the World Trade Center. The client didn't take any of the events into consideration or his own unwillingness to follow up on sales leads. Instead he tried to get out of paying my colleague his final payment. My colleague told the client he would send an e-mail to everyone he had contacted on the client's behalf to let them know what type of person they were dealing with. Fortunately, the client paid rather than be exposed.

3. "The market for your type of service has changed and I don't think I should have to pay so much." I couldn't believe my ears when a client told me that his spouse said the fee for my business plan development service should be less because the stock market had gone down and the demand for business plans had decreased as well. My head was ready to explode after he finished his lame excuse. I reminded him that he had signed a contract and that, if the demand for business plans had increased, he would be furious if, in the middle of my work, I told him that he had to pay more than we had agreed to or I wouldn't finish the project. The client knew he was wrong and said he had told his spouse it was wrong, but wanted to see what my reaction would be.

4. "I found a lot of errors in your document." A client called me on New Year's Eve to let me know that the document I had sent him had seven grammatical errors out of 6,250 words. That barely comes out to a tenth of a percent, and four of those so-called errors weren't errors.

5. "I don't like your writing style." As I am writing this book, a client told me he didn't want to pay the remaining part of my fee because he didn't like my writing style. Before he hired me, I gave him three samples of what I would do for him, plus a copy of each of my books. The client rewrote exactly 410 words out of 7,250. I told him that I had shown what I wrote and what he wrote to the person they were trying to impress without telling the person who had written what. The person rendering judgment picked my work over the client's work. Even after hearing that the person he was trying to impress had said he preferred my writing style to his, he is still withholding my final payment.

6. "A friend told me this project should have been done in a different way." I have yet to find the client who knows more about my area of expertise than I do, yet, for some reason, clients will ask a friend's opinion about the work I am doing. I don't mind constructive criticism, but I do mind when amateurs are asked to pronounce judgment on work they know little about.

I have had this happen to me and I have seen this happen to others. Once I almost became the friend asked to pass judgment, but, before I answered my friend's request, I told him I was not an expert and that, in my opinion, he should ask another expert before withholding payment.

7. "You took too long to get this done." Never in all the time I have been a consultant have I missed a deadline.

8. "The final product was different than what I expected." A friend of mine is a Web-site developer and he was asked to develop a Web site to promote a professional speaker's books and tapes. My friend kept her client informed every step of the way. When the site was completed, the client didn't like the overall product and refused to pay. My friend took the client to small claims court and won the case, but the client is appealing. Now my friend is considering dropping the suit and absorbing the loss.

9. "My boss doesn't like what you have done, so we aren't going to pay you." In Chapter 12, I wrote that you need to understand and fulfill the expectations of the person writing the check for your work. A *Fortune* 1000 company hired a colleague of mine to develop an e-commerce Web site. He followed my advice and asked to meet the check writer. The person he was dealing with said the boss didn't feel it was necessary and that they trusted the conduit's judgment. When the project was completed and unveiled to the boss, the boss told his employee that he was "underwhelmed" and refused to sign off on it. My colleague learned a very tough lesson.

10. "We have run out of money." Never take on a client who has less money than you do. This mostly applies to startups, but there are sizable companies that will tell consultants that they have exceeded their budget and may not have money in the next budget to pay them.

Professional Advice on Collecting Debts

If a client doesn't want to pay you, you have a variety of options, ranging from withholding the finished product, to threatening to expose their deceit, to suing them.

- **Withhold the finished product:** This works in the information technology field because, if you don't finish the programming, the application doesn't work. Unfortunately, in most cases, the consultant has provided enough that the client may be able to finish the project on their own.

- **Threaten to expose their deceit:** A colleague of mine who provides public relations asked a client three times to honor their agreement. The client refused and my colleague sent e-mails to all of us letting us know what happened. Being a consultant, I felt for him and wrote to the client on his behalf, encouraging him to honor the contract if everything that was written was true. The client had underestimated my colleague. He sent him a check, but told him he would never use him again. My colleague wrote back that the operative word was *used* and that he wouldn't let himself be used again.

- **Sue the client:** Unless the fee is over $50,000, you will find that suing someone will cost more money

Write It Off

A client I developed a business plan for refused to pay me the stock that he owed me in his company five months after the project ended, because his new board was unhappy with the work and had instructed him not to pay me. I showed the work to two venture people who had liked the plan, and they said they would support my claim. My attorney said the amount of stock wasn't worth suing over and to write it off as a bad debt. The lesson learned is: even when you are right you can still lose.

than collecting it, and there is always the chance that you will lose.

I interviewed Dave Dessen, the Managing Partner of Dessen, Moses and Sheinoff, a law firm that specializes in collecting bad debts. Dave is a graduate of Temple University's School of Law. I asked him what consultants should do to protect themselves.

Question: When should you contact a lawyer about collecting debts owed to you?

Response: Allow 90 to 120 days after the bill is overdue. This assumes that the consultant has an internal process for collecting.

Question: For what amount of debt does it make sense to contact an attorney?

Response: A minimum of $1,000. Under that it isn't economically worthwhile.

Question: How much does it typically cost to engage an attorney to collect debt?

Response: Most attorneys do it on a contingency basis. The percentage ranges from 25 to 33 percent. For a collection agency it is higher. If the creditor wants to file suit, it has pay for the court costs. In this arrangement the lawyer doesn't charge an hourly fee for his or her time.

Question: What process does an attorney go through to collect the debt?

Response: The attorney gets supporting documentation and the debtor's last known address from the creditor. The lawyer then writes a letter. If the letter comes back as a bad address, then we have to track the debtor down. Usually, the lawyer will try letters first and then telephone calls. If the debtor continues to ignore letters and phone calls, then the creditor has to decide whether he wants to continue to pursue the person and, possibly, file suit.

Question: What are the chances of collecting the entire debt?

Response: It depends on the debtor. If the business isn't on the ropes, you probably will collect the entire debt. If the business is going into bankruptcy, then you probably won't collect the whole amount. Many times you can put the person on a payment plan. If personalities are involved, it could take a lot longer.

Question: Should you accept a payment schedule?

Response: You don't want to accept a payment schedule that goes on forever. If they are talking eight months to a year, that is reasonable. Once you are talking about more than a year, then it becomes problematic, and you probably don't want to agree to that.

Question: Do different states have different laws about collecting business debts?

Response: Yes! You need to speak to a lawyer in the state where the debtor resides. There are different rules and remedies in each state.

Question: What is the hardest part about collecting debt?

Response: One part is tracking the debtor down. Once you have gotten a judgment, it is sometimes difficult to find the assets to cover the debt.

Question: How much of my time will the attorneys need when collecting the debt?

Response: Very little! They will need someone to send the paper work to collect. If a suit is filed and there is a hearing, then the creditor will have to send someone to testify.

Question: What advice do you have about screening clients that lessens the chances of having to take a client to court?

Response: You can try to get a Dun & Bradstreet report. You can try to get a personal guarantee from the owner. You should send periodic bills, as opposed to one large bill at the end. If you have trouble getting those paid, then you have to question whether you want the client.

Chapter Key Points

- Unfortunately, business is full of dishonest people. Be prepared to get a little bruised and taken advantage of. Try to protect yourself by doing the following:
  - Make sure your contracts are unambiguous.
  - Make sure the check signer has reviewed and approved every step of the project.
  - Make sure the client has the financial wherewithal to pay you.
  - Hire a good debt-collection firm.
- If a client takes advantage of you, don't beat yourself up or waste a lot of time and energy trying to collect unless the sum of money is significant ($25,000 to $50,000). Just move on.

CHAPTER 16

DIFFERENT WAYS TO MAKE MONEY

MULTIPLE STREAMS OF INCOME

Practically every consultant I have ever met has limited his or her income by focusing only on providing his or her expertise in the form of project work. When I meet with fellow consultants and they ask me how I manage to make good money regardless of economic conditions, I tell them that I do it by diversifying. I believe you should leverage everything you know and can do, which will translate into more consulting opportunities and new sources of revenue that make you less dependent on fixed-price and per-hour-charged projects.

When I started consulting, I listed everything I thought I was good at and what friends and business associates told me I was good at. My skills are as follows:

- *writing*
- *networking*
- *speaking*
- *investigating*
- *thinking creatively*
- *managing people*

How to Develop Ideas for New Revenue Sources

My wife tells me that one of my strengths is coming up with new ideas. She believes it is one of my gifts, but I think everyone can do it if they open their eyes and ears. Here are some sources I use for coming up with ideas for new revenue:

- **Analyst Reports.** I like to read stock analyst reports from brokerage houses such as ETrade, (www.etrade.com) and Merrill Lynch (www.merrill.com) and research reports from organizations such as the Gartner Group (www.gartner.com). A great place to obtain research is Cyber Atlas (www.cyberatlas.com). I read in a research report that business professionals who buy products and services on the Internet typically spend under $200 a transaction, and many of those transactions are for a service such as travel and access to on-line databases for research and information. After reading this, I decided to develop two new ventures, one focused on helping organizations find speakers (www.freespeakers.org), the other helping new entrepreneurs start their ventures (www.bizlaunch.net).

- **Business Books.** I read a variety of business books, including autobiographies, biographies, and books on marketing and sales. I like reading books written by futurists like Faith Popcorn. I don't always believe or accept what futurists say, but they do give me ideas. I like reading biographies and autobiographies because ideas tried by legendary CEOs from the last century can still be applied in various ways today. What amazes me is how few businesspeople I know actually read anything besides magazines. Technology may change how businesses offer existing services or provide new opportunities, but the process and methodology of successful people are usually the same, and it's their stories that inspire new ideas.

- **Business Conferences.** One of the best ways to come up with new ideas is to attend venture capital and industry conferences. I particularly like venture capital conferences, because the companies that are presenting are typically focused on solving a particular problem that they have identified. It's interesting to hear what venture capitalists have to say about companies and which ones they decide to invest in.

  I read a variety of general business magazines, such as *Fast Company, Inc, Success, Fortune,* and *Forbes,* plus industry- or profession-specific magazines such as *CIO, CFO, Direct Marketing News,* and *Interactive Week.* I like reading business magazines because I learn about new businesses and services that give me ideas about what I can offer.

- **Consultants.** As much as I can, I try to have breakfast or lunch with other consultants to see what they are doing, how we can work together, and what new sources of income they have come up with. I ran into a consultant in New York who said he surveys a core of 30 professionals in his industry about different topics and e-mails that information to clients and prospects. I asked him if he ever thought of performing the same interviews for his clients and he said no, but it gave me an idea for a new service that I could offer.

- **Surveys.** Industry surveys are very telling about what people want and don't want. I like to visit the Web sites of trade associations and read the surveys they conduct. I also like to go on the U.S. Census site

> *I was at a sports marketing conference produced by the SRI Institute in New York, and I was listening to a description of the new concepts the sports establishment is selling as sponsorships to corporations. I got an idea for a service to attract and retain bank customers based on an idea that I heard at that conference. I am now talking to five banks that are interested in the idea.*

(www.census.gov), which provides a lot of insights into where business is going.

- **Web Sites.** Most people surf the Web for relaxation, but I like to type in the names of industries and corporate leaders in those industries to see what new products and services they are announcing and what types of people they want to hire.

Ten New Sources of Income

Once I made a list of my skills and what I like to do, I developed a list of the various ways I could make money and I began to leverage my skills, which helped me expand my sources of revenue. Here are the various ways I have made additional income. All of these sources have fed me new opportunities for my core consulting business.

1. Book Author. Writing a book requires a lot of time and discipline. Besides writing this book, I have written four other books: *Power Networking*, published by NTC Publishing, a division of McGraw-Hill, in 1997; *Small Business Turnaround*, published by Adams Media in 1999; *Financing and Building an E-Commerce Venture*, published by Prentice Hall in 2001; and *Web Sites Built to Last*, published by Adams Media in 2002.

My publishers have paid me approximately $50,000 up front, plus average royalties of 10 percent. The books have not only opened up new sources of revenue, but have given me a competitive advantage when I approach new clients because they demonstrate my level of expertise.

2. Board Seats. Because of my books and business contacts, I have been asked to sit on a variety of for-profit and non-profit business boards. The for-profit boards either give you shares of stock for your advice, expertise, and contacts or

> *The great thing about writing books is that you have the opportunity to meet a lot of people and those people sometimes lead to new business opportunities. One of the people I interviewed for one of my books invited me to sit on the board of directors and I received 10,000 shares of stock. The company is still in existence and, once the market turns around, my stock might be worth something.*

allow you to buy shares cheaply. I am on the boards of six companies. Recently, I was offered $2 a share for 20,000 shares of stock I received in compensation for my assistance.

3. Business Referrals. As a consultant, you are always networking to find new opportunities. One of the ways I have been able to make additional income is by making introductions on behalf of my clients to other clients and prospects. I ask for 10 percent of the gross revenue on any introduction I make that leads to new business. I receive my compensation once the company is paid. Over the last five years, I have made $70,000 through business introductions.

4. Employment Referrals. Because I have a large network of contacts, I receive many resumes from friends, clients, and business associates. If I come across someone I think is a fit for a client, I will ask the client if they will give me a recruiting fee if the introduction leads to that person staying for a minimum of three months. My clients are glad to pay me this fee because they know I understand their business and culture and that my fee is a third of what professional recruiters charge. In the last year, I have made $10,000 in referrals.

5. Newspaper Column. One of the best ways to build your visibility is to write a newspaper column. The other great part of writing a newspaper column is that many daily and specialty weekly papers will pay for your expertise because you cost a fraction of what a full- or part-time reporter would cost. Over the last five years, I have made $10,000 from my columns, plus I have saved an average of $15,000 a year in fees to attend conferences. The net gain has been over $80,000.

6. New Ventures. Once I learn my client's business, or if I have an idea for a prospect, I write a one- or two-page description of my idea. My ideas always focus on either bringing in new business or reducing costs, which are at the top of any company's list, regardless of the current business climate. I came up with a concept that would help one of my bank clients attract and retain customers called Bizlaunch (www.bizlaunch.net). The client liked the idea so much that she paid me $100,000 and allowed me to resell the idea to other financial institutions and split the revenue from any new sales.

7. On-Line Sales. This is simple. Books have been written in every area of expertise. I signed up to be an Amazon.com affiliate and I have been selling both my books and other people's books on Web sites that I control. This has brought me another $2,000 over the last couple of years.

8. Outsource Management. Whatever consulting you offer, you can suggest to your clients and prospects that you could fulfill the role on a part-time basis without the company having to spend money on all the costs associated with a full-time employee. I provide prospective clients or existing clients with the chart shown in Figure 16-1 when pitching this idea.

I have had two clients hire me as an outsourced CEO and Chief Marketing Officer, and I have made a total of $100,000 over the last two years as a full-time (but temporary) employee.

9. Speaking. Most organizations are interested in experts who will speak for free, but there is a sizable number that will pay you to speak because of your expertise. If you write a book and/or newspaper column, you increase your chances of getting speaking engagements. Over the last five years, I have made $5,000 from speaking, but, more importantly, the contacts I made have led to new consulting contracts totaling over $100,000.

Manager (from Salary.com)		
Categories	Internal Employee	Kramer
Salary	$61,000	$42,000
Benefits (25%)	$15,250	0
Office Space	$5,250	0
Telephone	$1,200	0
Office Supplies	$600	0
Computer Equipment/ Software	$2,000	0
Conferences/Seminars	$1,000	0
Total Cash Outlay	$86,300	$42,000
Paying Unemployment	X	Not Applicable
Severance	X	Not Applicable
Cost of Hiring a New Employee	X	Not Applicable
Training a New Employee	X	Not Applicable
Nonmanager, Two Years Experience (Salary.com)		
Categories	Internal Employee	Kramer
Salary	$38,450	$42,000
Benefits (25%)	$9,613	0
Office Space	$5,250	0
Telephone	$1,200	0
Office Supplies	$600	0
Computer Equipment/ Software	$2,000	0
Conferences/Seminars	$1,000	0
Total Cash Outlay	$58,113	$42,000
Paying Unemployment	X	Not Applicable
Severance	X	Not Applicable
Cost of Hiring a New Employee	X	Not Applicable
Training a New Employee	X	Not Applicable

FIGURE 16-1. Demonstrating the value of a consultant

10. Surveys. Anytime you are being retained to do work, more than likely there is an opportunity to survey employees, clients, or prospects on the problems that the company is having or to find new opportunities for the company. Recently, I interviewed venture capital firms on behalf of one of my clients, an executive search firm, to find out how my client was perceived by VCs and what new services my client could offer.

During the course of the interviews, a couple of the venture funds asked me if I would do this type of work for them, so I created a service called "Venture Capital Qualitative Audit." The mission of this service was to find out how the VC's portfolio companies are perceived by their clients, prospects, and former clients, which helps the VC determine if management is doing a good job and if the VC should continue to invest. Below is an example of the survey that I developed for VCs. Doing this for companies has brought in over $150,000 over the last four years.

Venture Capital Qualitative Survey

Process

We will interview a maximum of 30 individuals, unless otherwise specified by the Venture Fund. Our audit is divided into four parts:

- portfolio company interviews
- companies that chose someone else
- dissatisfied former portfolio companies
- board members who sat with fund representatives on portfolio company boards

The client can decide how to spread out the interviews, and could decide only to interview clients or a combination of clients and dissatisfied customers. If the client wants more people interviewed, we will adjust the price accordingly.

The client will supply the names, company name, telephone, and e-mail addresses of those individuals who will be interviewed. It has been my experience that the client should provide more names than we need to interview. For example, if the client wants me to interview 10 companies, then I need 20 contacts.

Depending on people's travel schedules and ability to return calls and set up interview times, the process usually takes four to six weeks. I am willing to conduct interviews any time from Sunday through Friday. I don't work Saturdays.

All interviews are conducted by telephone.

Report

The report will contain my conclusions regarding what I have learned, and unedited quoted comments without attribution. If I come across a client who is planning to end the relationship with the portfolio company and hasn't told the company, I will ask if I can pass that information along. If the interviewee says no, then I can't. Confidentiality is important.

Cost

The cost for the first audit would be $5,000 up front and nonrefundable, and another $5,000 if the information brought back was considered valuable. After the first audit, the pricing would be $5,000 up front and $5,000 on delivery. If the client wants more interviews, I will adjust the price accordingly. I do not charge for telephone calls or for putting together the reports.

Portfolio Client Questions

Market Awareness and Perceived Value

1. How did you hear about the fund?
2. Why did you accept investment in the fund?
3. Did the fund meet your expectations or fall short?

Quality of Fund Support

1. Who represented the fund on your board?
2. Was he or she knowledgeable about your business?
3. Did he or she take the time to understand your business?
4. Did he or she provide good suggestions about how to improve the business in the areas of operations, sales, marketing, or finding additional capital?
5. Did he or she open doors with other portfolio companies to bring in business or expertise?

Competition

1. What other funds did you consider?

2. Why didn't you choose one of them?

3. Whom do you view as the leader in this space?

Competitive Advantages

1. What are the strengths of the fund?

2. What areas could it improve on?

Understanding Company's Pain

1. What is your biggest day-to-day concern?

2. What could the fund do to enhance your chances of success?

Dissatisfied Portfolio Companies

Market Awareness and Perceived Value

1. How did you hear about the fund?

2. Why did you accept investment in the fund?

3. Did the fund meet your expectations or fall short?

Quality of Fund Support

1. Who represented the fund on your board?

2. Was he or she knowledgeable about your business?

3. Did he or she take the time to understand your business?

4. Did he or she provide good suggestions about how to improve the business in the areas of operations, sales, marketing, or finding additional capital?

5. Did he or she open doors with other portfolio companies to bring in business or expertise?

Competition

1. What other funds did you consider?

2. Why didn't you choose one of them?

3. Whom do you view as the leader in this space?

Competitive Advantages

1. What are the strengths of the fund?

2. What areas can it improve on?

Understanding Company's Pain

1. What could the fund do to enhance your chances of success?

2. Would you recommend the fund to other companies?

Deal Conduit Interviews (Accountants, Attorneys, and Investment Bankers)

1. Do you recommend companies to the fund?
2. What do you perceive as the fund's investment interests?
3. What do you perceive as the fund's strengths?
4. What areas could the fund improve on?
5. Is the fund responsive to you when you send them a deal?
6. When you see a good deal, which venture fund do you contact first on behalf of a client or prospect?
7. Which ventures in your region do you consider top tier?
8. What makes one fund better than another fund?
9. What are the traits of a quality venture capitalist?
10. What venture capitalist do you admire the most and why?

Board Member Questions

1. Who represents the fund on the board you serve?
2. What value does he or she contribute?
3. What do you perceive as the fund's strengths?
4. What areas could the fund improve on?
5. Is the fund responsive to you when you send them a deal?
6. When you see a good deal, which venture fund do you contact first on behalf of a client or prospect?
7. Which ventures in your region do you consider top tier?
8. What are the traits of a quality venture capitalist?
9. What venture capitalist do you admire the most and why?
10. Would you recommend this fund to other companies that are looking for capital?

Chapter Key Points

- One of the most valuable lessons I have learned is that you shouldn't rely solely on your expertise and the service you provide to be a successful consultant. I would say that 20 to 30 percent of my income has come from sources of revenue not directly related to what I do on a daily basis as a consultant.

- Follow these suggestions to come up with additional ways to earn income:
  - Attend industry and venture capital conferences.
  - Read business books and magazines.
  - Read surveys.
  - Read industry reports.
  - Review Web sites.

- Don't hesitate to charge your clients for introductions you can make to new contacts.

- Leverage your knowledge into opportunities for speaking, writing, and advisory opportunities.

INDEX